Clifford's Bay

An Island, a Dog, and a Morgan Horse

By Nancy J. Bailey

1

Clifford's Bay

Nancy J. Bailey

For Amanda

My Blood Sister.

List of Illustrations

Chapter One

Scorch and Cajun

Chapter Five

Ripple

Chapter Ten

Clifford Takes a Break

Chapter Fifteen

Clifford

Chapter Sixteen

Spirit Bird

Books by Nancy J. Bailey

The Clifford Horse Stories

Book 1: Clifford of Drummond Island

Book 2: Return to Manitou

Book 3: Clifford's Bay

My Best Cat

Holding the Ladder

The Horses Who Inspired Me

Acknowledgements

To Ms. Rip, the "sympathy dog", who knew her job from the beginning and does it well.

Thank you to my brothers, Jon, Ted and Dan, who are always there for me.

Thank you to Judy, my sister.

With thanks and love to the Cliffy Listers, who have held my hand through it all.

To my friend Beth Duman who "can see that there's a light in me."

To Kristi Misiak who has that rare and wonderful talent of making me laugh until I cry.

To Vickie Sheathelm, the one who walked in when others were walking out.

To Jack who answered my SOS.

To Claire, who is always up for anything, and has given me a soft place to land.

With special love and hugs to Lori and Miracle Maxx.

To Julie Thrush, and her German Shepherds, Lacey, Falco, LaCrosse and Kian.

To Judy Long and Baroncrest Nuggeteer.

To Jim and Cindy, my friends and neighbors.

To Rose Wahl, who loved Cajun.

To Debbie Hendrikson and Becky, the spunky West Highland White Terrier.

Thank you Anne and Rob Wyland, for hosting all the wonderful trail rides.

To Lori Pompili for keeping my spirits up with a steady supply of Jimmy Buffett.

To the Oncology staff of MSU Veterinary Teaching Hospital.

To the staff of Kern Road Veterinary Hospital.

To Walli who never stops believing in me.

And special thanks to my heavenly Father, whom I'm sure has a very good explanation for all of this.

bay

-noun

1. *A body of water forming an indentation of the shoreline, larger than a cove but smaller than a gulf.*

2. *In Zechariah 6:3, 7 bay denotes the color of horses, but the original Hebrew means strong, and is here used rather to describe the horses as fleet or spirited*

3. *The situation of a person or thing that is forced actively to oppose or to succumb to some adverse condition*

Chapter One

"Scorch! What a great name! How did he get it?" The young veterinary technician smiled, directing her gaze to the dog sitting at my feet.

I shrugged and grinned. "Well, just look at him!"

He was a mutt. He was half Australian shepherd, half mystery dog. He was sitting on the scrubbed tile floor, his reddish brown paws pointing carefully straight ahead so he didn't start to slip. His coat was mostly black, streaked with a mixture of ashy burnt splotches here and there. His ears were up and they tipped over in an alert flop, and his brown eyes snapped with intelligence. He was, as always, watching my face. With every word I spoke, his head tilted this way and

15

that. He had greeted the tech politely, but now ignored her as if she did not exist. He knew we were in the vet clinic. He didn't mind seeing the vet. He had walked in through the lobby, off leash, and hopped on the scale without bidding. He weighed 40 lbs. He'd had a cough for a couple of days and was not acting right. I was thinking maybe he needed antibiotics.

The tech was standing with a clipboard. "Okay, if you want to just wait here in the exam room, Dr. Woody will be right in."

She left the room. I noticed a canister of semi-moist liver treats on the counter, and pulled off the lid. Scorch's eyes brightened and he stood up and started panting happily.

"Give me a big smile," I whispered. His nose wrinkled, lips peeling back to reveal rows of bright teeth, baring a huge ugly grin. I tossed him a treat, which he caught deftly.

Everyone asked me why he was called Scorch. But from the first time I saw him in 1996, with his black coat and sooty grey markings, I knew his name. For nine years, he had shadowed me, always watchful. If I glanced down he was generally just a few feet away, and usually staring at me. I often wondered what it was about me that he found so interesting. But it was perhaps this vigilance that has created our effective communication. I might speak a few soft words, and he would go and immediately do as I asked. "Lie down." "Get your Kong." "Go tell Cajun it's time to go."

He did silly things to make me laugh. The more sophisticated the humor, the harder I laughed. He liked it that I got the joke, and he was constantly trying to upstage himself. He could pull my socks off, gently nibbling around my toes to grasp an edge, and then he pulled. If they were knee socks, or the especially clingy type, he braced himself and tugged full force. He never damaged the sock. When it finally peeled off my foot, he would carry it over and present it to me. He loved pulling socks off so much that sometimes he had to be dissuaded from doing it to others.

He humored his "brother", my German shepherd, Cajun. He was no match for the big dog's power and stamina, but took pleasure in tormenting him. We played a game I called, "Ball off the deck," in which I threw a ball from the deck and it bounced across the lawn. The dogs loved to run down the deck steps to chase the ball. They would take turns if necessary, but I often sent them together.

When I threw the ball, Cajun would shriek and leap after it, but Scorch stood and watched where it fell before running down the steps. Because of this, Scorch usually would be first to find the ball. He had learned that Cajun would bully him if he tried to carry it anywhere, so he didn't try to bring the ball back. He would pick it up and stand there, holding it while Cajun ran around the yard looking for it. Finally, Cajun would notice, and he'd pounce. Scorch would drop the ball, and when Cajun grabbed it, Scorch would quickly mount him from behind and start humping him ferociously.

Cajun had his mouth full, and he'd stand there snarling and growling. He couldn't bring the ball back, because then he'd be running away from Scorch, and not "man enough" to face up to this humiliation. He'd have liked to turn around and bite Scorch, but to do that, he'd have to drop the ball. He was not about to drop the ball. Cajun was stuck. Scorch knew this. So he locked on while Cajun snarled guttural, useless threats through his mouthful, just blissfully humping away.

Scorch especially loved doing this when we had company. When this happened in front of an audience, people were mortified. They immediately started yelling at Scorch, "Stop it! What's he DOING? Isn't he NEUTERED?"

I would be leaning on the deck rail, gasping for air, wiping away the tears. It killed me every time. "Yes!" I'd gasp, "He's neutered, he's been neutered for eight years." I realized that my hysterical laughter was only egging Scorch on, but I couldn't help it.

Scorch liked agility class, but he was not a jock. He liked to learn new stuff, but usually in the form of tricks or some type of problem that engaged his mind. He loved Kong toys and Buster Cubes. He was the master of the Kong, the hollow rubber toy that I filled with cheese and bits of liver. I would cram the Kong with biscuits and then pack every nook with smaller bits of bacon or jerky. Scorch could extricate any treat from the Kong, no matter how tightly it fit. If Cajun eventually gave up and left something rattling around in his Kong, Scorch would furtively steal it and clean it out. He was a problem solver.

He didn't want to fraternize with other dogs. He scorned them, always looking to me instead, to see what our next project might be.

"He's not like any other dog," our agility instructor told me, time and again. "Scorch is just not like any other dog."

Now he sat in the veterinarian's exam room, enthusiastically grimacing, baring his teeth, sneezing, waving his paw and going through various other acts in his attempt to prompt me to toss him another treat.

The door opened and Dr. Woody came in. She was a serious-faced kid, her red hair pulled back in a no-nonsense pony tail. But when she saw Scorch, she smiled and bent down to pet him. "Hello there."

"He's been coughing," I explained. It was our first time at Kern Road Clinic, which is just a few miles from our house. I didn't think it was anything serious, and Scorch didn't like to ride in the car, so I didn't haul him all the way back to Ann Arbor. It's an hour from the farm.

"He sure is tuned in to you," Dr. Woody said.

"I'm thinking about getting a T shirt that says, 'Scorch TV'," I quipped.

She laughed.

She ran her hands over Scorch's throat, and immediately her face became very serious. "I don't like this. His lymph nodes are swelling."

She stood up. "I want to do some bloodwork on him. But this isn't good. I can tell you right now that he has cancer."

The words came at me like a hammer. I stood there silently, while Dr. Woody explained that they would schedule surgery to remove one of the swollen nodes and confirm the diagnosis. It was a flood of confusing information: Lymphoma. Biopsy. Surgery. Alternatives. Chemotherapy. Life expectancy. Scorch watched me carefully. As I nodded my head while Dr.

Woody spoke, Scorch nodded his head too, so vigorously that his ears flipped.

"I'll take him in back and we'll do an X ray." Dr. Woody took a leash that hung on the wall and draped it around his neck. Scorch continued to watch me.

"Go ahead," I told him. He turned immediately and followed Dr. Woody out of the exam room.

As soon as he was gone, I felt myself beginning to panic. I was breathing hard. I grasped the cold metal edge of the exam table and stood there, hyperventilating. This news was totally unexpected. If he saw me like this, he would feel it too. I had to get this under control. I walked out of the exam room into the main lobby. It was large, sterile and empty, except for one receptionist behind the desk around the corner. There was a basket of dog toys by the window, and some benches lining the wall, and a movie playing on the TV.

I saw that the movie was "Babe", the sheep-herding pig story. It was one of my favorites, so I decided it would be a good idea to distract myself by watching for a moment.

That was a big mistake.

It was near the end, where the farmer and pig are finishing up the sheep herding trial and Babe goes and sits by his side. The farmer has that understated little grin, and soft praise, "That'll do, Pig. That'll do." And the look passes between them.

I was nearing total meltdown. I ran out to the truck, where Cajun waited, and let him out. I brought him into the clinic so he could wait with me.

All my anxiety transferred to him instantly. I was much calmer, but he whimpered and whined, sniffing Scorch all over when they brought him back. And then, when they took Scorch out again for yet more x rays, Cajun lay with his nose by the bottom of the door and started to wail.

"He's coming back," I said calmly. Cajun looked up at me, and then he relaxed.

And so did I. I had a few more emotional breakdowns over the next few days, but never in front of Scorch. The week that followed was all about Cancer. I couldn't think about anything else, and I am sure anyone who tried to talk to me was getting a vacant response, if any. By this time, I'd been divorced for four years. It was just me and the critters. Scorch had many friends, mostly through the internet, thanks to the relative notoriety of his "brother", Clifford the Morgan horse. I appreciated their support and empathetic comments about the diagnosis.

Scorch tested positive for lymphoma at Michigan State University the following Wednesday and had his first chemotherapy treatment. They kept him overnight for observation, just to be sure he wasn't going to have a bad reaction.

I opted for an aggressive form of treatment and he would be receiving chemotherapy over the next five months. Statistically there is a 95% success rate of remission. The tricky part is, they can't predict how long the remission will last.

The treatment was horrendously expensive, but I decided early on that money was not going to be an object. Scorch was nine years old, and that is way too young to lose a dog, especially a mixed breed dog that is supposed to have hybrid vigor. I began thinking about how to raise funds for his treatment. I opened an online store in Scorch's name, with products featuring my art work, thinking it might help.

I once had a friend tell me that for someone who has so much bad luck, I have really good luck. And in this case, it was true. Scorch came through his chemo with flying colors and was back home again the next day. He ate a big dinner. He was only too happy to come out and help me feed the horses. It was dark and the snow was falling softly. Scorch gobbled up huge bites of snow, just like always, and Cajun looked for sticks.

It was so good to have him back, behaving like his old self! My friend Debi Boies had suggested that I give him lots of encouraging pats and praise, just to show him I was okay with everything. I agreed with her, and I took it a step further. I threw my hands up in the air and started jumping up and down, shouting, "We did it! WE DID IT! We're ALIVE!! YAAAYYY!!!!" and the dogs jumped around too and bark excitedly. We all spent a few minutes together that evening, dancing and cavorting in the snow.

Chapter Two

Oh, you can depend on me
Over and over
Over and over
Know that I intend to be
The one who always makes you laugh until you cry
And you can call on me
Until the day you die

~ "You're a Friend of Mine", performed by
Clarence Clemons and Jackson Browne

I felt lucky to be living in close proximity to Michigan State University's school of veterinary medicine. Our oncologist was Dr. Dervisis, a gentle soul from Portugal, with big, brown limpid eyes.

In the waiting room, there was always a variety of people and pets, each in a different stage of their cancer journey. I was able to get to know a couple of them over the course of weeks, most especially Maxx, the Chemo Kitty.

Maxx was a grey tabby cat just under two years old. He was not happy about treatment. He stayed in his carrier with his blankie, so I never did get to know the "Real Maxx". His mom, Lori, would sit working on her knitting. She had driven all the way down from Traverse City, a journey of about three hours, every two weeks for Maxx's chemo treatment. Lori was tall and willowy, a friendly and beautiful woman. Her favorite color was green. She was always clad in green sweaters or t-shirts, and her knitting projects were often in various shades of lime or teal, lovingly pieced together and carried in a fabric bag. She usually brought her mom, Pat, to keep her company during the long wait in the MSU lounge. Lori had a fantastic memory for details. She always asked after other patients, how so-and-so was doing, how the kidney test results had turned out, and the like. Naturally, people warmed to her immediately. Scorch did, too. She began bringing treats for him and it didn't take him long to figure out that she kept them in her purse. He would greet her enthusiastically and then try to rifle through the handbag.

She taught him to take treats from her lips. It was one trick I hadn't thought of.

Scorch always performed in the waiting room, for the entertainment of patients and staff alike. The favorite trick was when he said his prayers. He'd put his front paws up on a chair and hide his eyes, until I said, "Amen."

My favorite trick was his "Speak." It had started out as a regular bark, but over time he turned it into something much more brilliant. I would say, "Speak!" and he'd throw his head back with a "Woof!" Then I would say, "Shhh... Too loud." He would throw his head back the same way, and a little squeak would come out. I would literally screech with laughter at this. I think the laughing reinforced him, because he eventually worked it out to the point where after I said, "Shhh," he would throw back his head, open his mouth, but no sound at all would come out. It cracked me up every time.

One day, while watching out shtick, Pat said, "He's such an unusual dog. Where did you find him?"

"He found me," I said. "I was at an adoption event trying to find a home for a foster dog. He just lay in the corner staring me all day. Then when the event was over, he walked across the room and put his paws up on me. I had to take him home."

"That gives me goosebumps," Pat said. She looked at him. "He really is not like any other dog."

Pet owners were not allowed to go back into the treatment room. So when his time came for treatment, the techs would come to get Scorch. He would go with them, but as they left, his tail would drop and his head would sink. He would walk very slowly out of the waiting room.

Scorch's cancer treatment was regarded with great interest and sympathy by the Morgan folks who knew Clifford. One friend in California, Lynn, said, "It seems to me that you communicate with your animals on a very high level. You should work on developing that."

I'd had an experience where an animal communicator had spoken with Clifford about his trailering issues. I didn't think I could possibly master this type of intuition, but I started investigating just out of curiosity. According to theory, most people have this ability, but they never develop it. Most pet owners "read" and "communicate" with their pets very well; they just don't realize they are doing it. While in the waiting room, I decided to try an experiment. Next to me, a little Bichon was sitting on its owners lap. It was panting pretty hard. I wondered if the dog lived with any other dogs, and got a clear picture of a black, brown and white Shih Tzu.

"What a sweet Bichon," I said to the man. "Do you have any other pets?"

"Oh yes, we have Davy," he said.

"What kind of dog is Davy?"

"Davy is a Shih Tzu. He's brown and white."

Now at the risk of really looking like an oddball, I asked, "But doesn't he have black on him?"

The man paused to think. "Oh yes, he has black on his ears."

My image was correct, but I shrugged it off, telling myself that a person with a Bichon was very likely to own another type of small dog.

Those of us who were in the waiting room shared the common experience of having a pet with cancer. Bodily functions were discussed with candor. Vomiting, diet, the color and texture of stools, were all topics readily examined. Dogs and cats usually handled chemo a lot better than people did. But one of the side effects of chemo, to my dismay, was chronic diarrhea.

"Boy, he's got to be miserable with it," I told Lori. "This morning he left a big puddle by the basement door. It was awful. It's like he tries to make it outside but he just can't."

She pointed her knitting needle at me. "Try canned pumpkin."

"Really?"

"Yes. It's great fiber. And Maxx loves it."

I became an advocate for holistic dog food and healthy supplements. Scorch was anemic, so I began buying beef liver at the grocery store and boiling it. He and Cajun both loved it. The second week of chemo was lots better, but he still seemed a little queasy. But he consumed two huge meals a day and especially enjoyed his canned pumpkin.

One afternoon, when I said the magic words, "Time to feed horses," he bounded up in excitement, knowing that he usually could cajole me into a walk then.

"It's cold out!" I groaned. But, having a dog with cancer meant it was time to Seize the Day. So, we did walk down the long driveway. I was bundled up in coat and hat, and scarf, and Scorch and Cajun sniffed and raced through mud and tall brown grass.

When Scorch hunched in the tall grass, I held my breath and waited. It was one of those moments only a dog owner can truly understand. Then, as I described it later, racquetballs came to mind. They were dark and hard and they even bounced! I ran over to them and said, "Scorch! Those are the most beautiful things I have ever seen! GOOD BOY!!!"

He pranced and panted and we continued our walk up the country road in a state of bliss. I was euphoric. Then the neighbor's van came pulling up and he rolled down the window, smiling. "Hey! What are you so excited about?"

I hesitated for a second. Then, oh what the heck. It was bubbling up, so I just let it out.

"HARD POOP!" I shouted.

He flinched.

"HARD POOP! HARD POOP!" I hopped up and down and whipped my hat off my head, flinging it up into the air just like Mary Tyler Moore. "We've got HARD POOP!"

And Scorch was jumping around too, barking his funny squeaky bark, but I swear he was saying, "POOP! POOP! POOP!"

The neighbor laughed, looked around and then quickly pulled away.

Chapter Three

Dr. Dervisis had given Scorch a prognosis of roughly eight months in remission with treatment. After only four months, in July, Scorch relapsed and the cancer was back. It was discovered on his spleen during a routine ultrasound. We again opted for aggressive treatment and planned to have the spleen removed.

During those days, Scorch would occasionally come over, rest his head on my knee, and give me a look. I didn't like it when he did this. It felt like he was trying to tell me goodbye.

"I don't want to hear it," I would say. "You are going to be fine."

With the surgery date pending, I decided we all needed a break from the cancer lifestyle. It was time to go to Drummond Island. I hitched up Wheelzebub, my passive-aggressive red horse trailer, and loaded Clifford, my Morgan gelding. Clifford was a deep red chestnut with a white blaze on his face. The blaze was in the shape of an exclamation mark, which was a succinct and accurate statement about his personality. He was fourteen years old that year, and had been traveling in trailers all his life. He climbed in willingly enough, but he had to travel in Wheelzebub alone because he was claustrophobic. So I moved the partition over and he immediately swung his rump around to stand sideways. He rolled his eye at me as I swung the back doors shut.

My other Morgan, Clifford's sister Trudy, was a dark bay mare who didn't like being left alone. Fortunately, we had a visitor that summer. Trudy and Clifford's sister, Kerry Arabesque, better known as Peaches, was spending some time with us. Neither mare even looked up while the dogs climbed in the truck, and we took off on our five hour journey north.

Some of my friends protested that Scorch should be kept quiet, that his cancer would spread if he moved around too much. But I felt that the more he moved, the stronger he would be, and the stronger he was, the better his immune system would be. The MSU oncologists found a few bad cells in his blood, but thought it may not have spread to the bone marrow. I remembered when my German Shepherd, Reva, at age twelve, needed to have her spleen removed. She suffered no ill effects afterward, and she went on to live for three more years.

Drummond Island, the "Gem of the Huron", rests in the Saint Marie's River, a freighter's passageway between the freshwater seas known as Superior and Huron. I had grown up there, and spent every summer there since getting Clifford some thirteen years prior.

Every afternoon Cajun, Scorch and I were walking two miles, from my Dad's camp in the woods, out to the shores of Huron Bay, and then two miles back.

The dogs were elated to be back. Scorch was so happy! When I threw the stick, he attacked his brother ferociously like usual, jumping and snarling at him as Cajun raced off to get it.

He was never crazy about swimming, but we were having a record-breaking heat wave. The dogs and I went in the water. The clear Lake Huron wavelets lapped gently around my feet, thirstily touching the flat rocky shore. I had some rubber shoes that I wore on the rocks to keep me from slipping, and I'd wade out to my knees and throw sticks out for the dogs. When Scorch brought his stick back, his legs would get all rubbery. He was sort of paddling around me, although he could walk. I got down and rubbed him and he just kind of floated there, so happy in his weightlessness.

The unique ambience of Drummond: the twisted cedars, the soft murmur of the poplar leaves in the summer heat, the bursting orange-red of the wild tiger lilies, had such a calming effect on me. I felt my anxiety melting away.

Scorch had no interest in going on rides with Clifford. I didn't make him go. He opted to stay at camp. Clifford would trot all the way down to the fork that led to Clifford's Bay, and always, always he would try to veer off that way.

"Not this time," I would tell him, and we would turn the other way. The bay was my ancestor's landing place, our special sand beach. It was slated for development, so I had been avoiding it that year. We had ridden there every summer, and the horses had run loose on the shore, reveling in the sun and the warm sand. To think of it being all torn up was unbearable.

For me, the one other thing that would make our summer better was if the whole family could be reunited. I missed Trudy something fierce.

Peaches was due to be shipped to her new home in Washington State, so when the time came for Scorch to have his surgery, I hauled Wheelzebub back down to pick up Trudy. The surgery went well, and we stayed for a few days to let Scorch recover. Then we loaded up Trudy and headed North.

When she was released at camp, she jumped out of the trailer and ran to Clifford, and the two of them stood still for the longest time with their heads together, blowing into each other's nostrils in an equine greeting.

Then, three weeks after his spleen was removed, Scorch was back to his old self. He became very excited one midsummer afternoon when he saw I had my riding pants on. When I finally swung aboard Trudy, he was jumping around barking, but I thought he was just going to see us off, trotting out to the road and then turning back, like he had been doing that year.

But when he saw Clifford trotting loose after us, he started doing his bop-down-the-road, looking over his shoulder, leading and encouraging Clifford like he used to do. We were all together! We were going to the beach!

For the first time all year, we rode the two miles down to Clifford's Bay. Scorch's excitement, and the temptation to let Clifford run loose on the shore again, were just too overwhelming to ignore. Clifford's Bay was one of the few sand beaches on the rocky island. It was a little inlet surrounded by cedars, with a creek that tumbled down over the rocks and emptied into the bay. There was a gravel shoal about fifty yards offshore where the gulls rested, and errant wildflowers popped their heads out. Sandpipers ran along the water's edge, and loons bobbed farther out in the bay. The horses loved the beach. They took turns running loose on the shoreline, rolling in the sand and splashing in the bay.

It was a wonderful, golden afternoon, with columns of clouds piling up on the horizon, a perfect summer day. The dogs ran in the sand and splashed in the shallows. Clifford was in rare form: Bucking, crow hopping, snorting and playing.

That day, on the way back, we came to a spot in the road where Clifford, if he was running loose like this, always tried to scare me. Usually it was in the form of an ambush. This time he came galloping up from behind, straight at Scorch. Scorch didn't appear to see him coming, and he just stood there sniffing something in the grass. I held my breath and did not call out, because I was worried he would focus on me then, and not what was going on. He was in a spot where it wasn't going to be easy to get out of the way, right between Trudy and the trees.

Clifford blasted up with his ears pinned. Normally in a case like this, he would lower his head and butt the dog out of the way. I watched in horror as he just kept coming. At the last possible moment, he rose up, folding his front legs neatly, sailing through the air in a spectacular jump right over Scorch.

"Damn you, Clifford!" I screeched.

He hit the ground on the other side of the dog, who wasn't moving, and then flicked his tail and ran on up the trail.

He had gotten me again. As he trotted away, he twirled his head with pride.

Chapter Four

I'll be fine, yes
'Cause you're a friend of mine

~ "You're a Friend of Mine", performed by
Clarence Clemons and Jackson Browne

Scorch and I were in the waiting room at MSU, working on a new trick as we waited for test results. I was teaching him to do a Spanish walk, like an Andalusian horse. Scorch had been trained with a clicker, a small plastic noisemaker that signaled "yes" to him. A click meant food was coming. I didn't want to use a clicker in the waiting room, thinking the noise would be disruptive. With Scorch, I had long since replaced the click with the word, "Yes". So I was just softly saying the word, "Yes," and then giving him bits of liver from my fanny pack. It was taking all his concentration to learn the walk. He had to first stretch one foot forward, then the other. It was difficult for him, because he had a strong compulsion to do his, "walking on three legs" trick. He wanted to hold up one foot and hop on the other. He was having to unlearn that to learn this new thing. He was panting hard, and he was pretty consistently giving me three steps in succession, right on the verge of a breakthrough.

Just then, man came in with a very noisy, lunging boxer. The waiting room was full. Scorch and I retreated to the corner and he lay down near my feet. The boxer was on the other side of the room, but he was very excited, leaning on his leash and gasping, wheezing loudly.

The other animals in the room, including Maxx the Chemo Kitty, were all completely silent and civilized. The one creature disrupting this was the obnoxious boxer. "GASP! GASP!"

Finally, Scorch seemed unable to take it anymore. He stood up and glared at the boxer. He barked angrily three times. Then he lay down again. Lori and I burst out laughing.

"Well, if I've ever heard a dog cuss, that was it," Lori said.

"No kidding!" I said. "This is a HOSPITAL, for criminy's sake! That guy needs to show some respect!"

Dr. Dervisis appeared. He looked at me. "We need to talk about Scorch's test results." Lori and Pat, who were sitting with me in the waiting room, drew a collective deep breath as I followed him into an exam room. I handed Scorch's leash to Lori as I passed.

Dr. Dervisis closed the door, turned around to face me and said, "Scorch's cancer is back."

I sat down.

"We need a different type of chemotherapy. I want to try a more aggressive form of treatment, called DTIC, that would require him to be on an IV drip for eight hours."

"Would I be allowed to sit with him during the eight hours?"

He shook his head. "I'm sorry. Unfortunately, we do not allow owners to be present when chemotherapy is administered, due to the biohazard of the treatment."

I shifted uncomfortably. "Well... How many treatments would be required?"

"The number of treatments depends on the response we see. The question to be answered first is if the chemo is going to work. If it works, then we use it for as long as it is efficacious. This is generally the plan for any type of rescue chemotherapy for lymphoma in dogs." Then he added, "In humans they do rescue chemo to put them in complete remission and then go for bone marrow transplant."

I came out of the room. Scorch was sitting by Lori with his head in her lap. He looked up at me, panting happily.

"The cancer is back," I said.

"Oh no!" Lori said. "I'm so sorry! What are you going to do?"

"I'm not sure yet. I have to think about this."

We promptly headed back to Drummond. I was beside myself. I was going into a financial hole. I was paying what I could on my credit cards, but it was a struggle. Michigan's economy was the worst in the nation and there were no jobs, especially for someone like me who had been out of the mainstream work force for so many years. Art sales were hitting the skids.

My best friend of 23 years, Kimmy, had died two years prior of cirrhosis of the liver. Her mom, Janice, still lived up in her hometown of Manistique. I talked with Janice on the phone every so often. She said Scorch was on the prayer chain at her church. "When we Baptists pray, we PRAY," she said. "But you need to remember the Serenity Prayer."

I remembered it.

God, grant me the serenity to accept
the things I cannot change,
The courage to change the things I can,
And the wisdom to know the difference.

I thought the last part was where I had the most trouble.

If I thought the chemo would help him, I would have found a way to do it. Even though Scorch loved seeing Lori and the other regulars at MSU, and loved performing his tricks in the waiting room, he hated the chemo. Every time the techs led him back there, his head and tail would droop, and he would go reluctantly along. I could not possibly ask him to sit in a cage with an IV drip for eight hours.

My little sister Amanda had taken to hanging around with me during my days on the Island. Amanda was a riot. She had Down's syndrome and used it to disguise her wicked humor from the world.

One evening I was making a pot of chili. Just to see her reaction, while adding ingredients I took a cup of dog food and acted like I was going to dump it in.

"Oh, come on now," she said. "I don't need no shiny coat!"

She made some comment that evening about Cajun. "He'll have a long life."

"Well, Scorch will too," I said.

She was silent.

It wasn't good. Amanda knew things. It was difficult to explain. She was connected spiritually in a way that few people are. She talked about people she knew that had passed on, like Kimmy and our grandparents. She was a little obsessed with them. Most of the family members didn't pay attention to this. After all, she had Down's. That set her apart to begin with.

But I knew that to underestimate Amanda usually meant that I'd be missing out on something. One day, she was talking about Linda, a friend of mine from Arizona. Linda had been killed in an accident in the 80's. Amanda had never met her.

"Linda said hi."

"Are you talking to the dead again?"

"I don't talk to them. They talk to me."

"Oh, okay."

Suddenly, she started to laugh. "Linda was talking about Clifford. Linda really likes Clifford!"

This got my attention. Linda was a fun-loving girl with two horses of her own. She had a wicked sense of humor. Linda would have definitely appreciated my equine practical joker, Clifford.

I decided to do a little test. "Hey Amanda, next time you talk to Kimmy, I want you to ask her something. Can you do that for me?'

"Okay."

"When Kimmy was a kid, she had a dog named Cookie. Ask her why she named that dog Cookie."

Cookie had been a white collie. She was thus named because she had a round brown spot on her side, perfectly resembling a cookie.

I reminded Amanda a couple more times that day. "Remember to ask Kimmy why she named her dog Cookie."

The next day, I asked Amanda. "Did you talk to Kim? Did you ask about Cookie?"

"Oh. Yes." Amanda rolled her eyes upward, as one does when they are trying to remember something. I thought there were plenty of potential answers for the question. Maybe the dog was sweet. Maybe the dog loved cookies. Maybe the dog was found as a puppy eating a box of vanilla wafers. The possibilities were endless.

Finally, Amanda took a deep breath. "It's because the dog is round and brown."

A chill shot through me. I knew there was something odd going on, but I didn't expect Amanda's answer to be so on target. It was enough to convince me that Amanda was privy to things most people weren't. So I asked her again about Scorch.

"So, Scorch is going to be okay, right?"

She said nothing.

"Amanda?"

"I don't want to say." She wouldn't look at me.

I decided not to push it, but I wasn't giving up hope. I started investigating alternative treatments for Scorch. I felt like I was heading into a long corridor, from which there was no turning back. I prayed for guidance. I had said a prayer to God to speak to me through animals, since these are the only things I seem to consistently notice and listen to.

As we took our walks, during the following days, a number of hawks appeared. One flew over us with a mouse in its claws, and another one Cajun chased up from the road.

I knew that hawks were considered spiritual messengers. I thought maybe the next animal I encountered was going to tell me something. I hoped it would be a deer, the totem animal of dreams. That might mean the answer was coming in a dream, which might be simple and cool.

But I didn't see any deer that night. I didn't see any wild mammals at all. The path as always was littered with tons of butterfly escorts, in all sizes and colors. That night, I heard coyotes wailing just before I went to sleep. I must have fallen asleep to them because I couldn't remember when it ended.

The next day I looked up coyote totems and wasn't too happy with what I found. They are bearers of mischief and you can be prepared for Murphy's Law when they are your messengers!

"NO," I thought. "No more Murphy's Law. No more disasters, please!"

Kimmy's death had been a hard loss and I still was reeling from the shock of it. The economy was getting worse and I was starting to worry about how I was going to keep the farm. I didn't want any more crises in my life.

Then on my walk that day, I noticed a butterfly sitting on a stalk of goldenrod beside the road. As I approached, it didn't fly away. I thought that odd, so bent to take a look. It was a dark brown one with white stripes on the wings -- very striking. As I examined it I noticed that it had apparently been battered, and the lower half of its right wing was gone, leaving tatters along the edge.

Now I knew why it didn't fly! "Poor thing," I said. And then it took off! It flew up over my head, made a circle, and then went up and landed high above on some spruce needles.

I gasped. I stood there in the road, just looking at that butterfly, and thinking that it was an encouraging sign.

The summer was aging gracefully, the days turning toward frost at night. Scorch was feeling good enough to continue our walks, though he had given up on trail rides. He was fat, since the prednisone had made him hungry all the time, but he was in good condition from all the activity. The months of chemo had taken their toll though, as his muzzle had gone completely grey and his eye had that aged look that belongs to a wise old dog. As the weeks passed, he began to move more slowly. At night, he would lie in his bed in the corner. If I sighed, or took a deep breath, so did he. I wondered how long we had been breathing together.

He was due for more blood work, so we took another trip south. Meanwhile, I started investigating a product called Cantron. It was invented by a researcher who spent forty years developing it. It was reputed to be 80% effective. The theory was that cancer grows so fast, requiring so much energy, the body is overworked struggling to feed it. Cantron lowers the overall energy of the body. The cancer dies from energy starvation and the dead cells are flushed from the body.

A court injunction had shut down the researcher's efforts, but there was still an underground group promoting Cantron. They sold it for what it cost to make. It was a little like bootlegging, except they didn't seem to be in it for profit. I called the local group leader, Chuck, who had a raspy voice like an old farmer.

"What do you want the Cantron for?" he asked.

"It is for my dog, who has been in chemo at MSU but I have discontinued chemo."

"That was a good idea," he said casually. "We have dogs getting over cancer all the time."

He wanted me to come to the monthly meeting which is the second Tuesday of November, but I told him that Scorch's appetite was starting to wane and I was concerned that he wouldn't make it that long.

So he gave me another contact number and I went to pick up the magic potion.

It was Scorch's worst day so far. He didn't want to eat that morning, but finally was coaxed into taking some chicken. The day prior, he had participated in a Frisbee game and actually caught it, twice. But today, although his eyes lit up, he would rather sit back and smile and let Cajun play with the Frisbee. He was walking around like an old man and didn't want to leave the house.

That night, while on my way home from a friend's house about midnight, a big buck threatened to cross the road in front of me. I slowed immediately but he carried out his threat. I slammed on the brakes and skidded, stopping just after I clobbered him and knocked him down. He sprawled out on the road, got up and walked away.

When I got home, I surveyed the damage. The car was dinged all over the front corner panel, one ding on the hood, and the side view mirror was knocked out. There was deer hair sticking here and there. Scorch got out of the car and sniffed all over where the deer had impacted.

I found out that the thing to do was make a police report, so I called the next morning, only to be told that the area where the deer was hit was not covered by any police units and the state police had to be called in. I called, and waited, and nobody showed up so I left. I had to go get Scorch's potion and then go to the vet clinic for more Prednisone.

While I was at the clinic, my cell phone rang. Sure enough, it was the dispatcher informing me that the police officer was driving around looking for my house.

"Just tell him to come to the veterinary clinic," I said. "It's a lot easier to find. I'll wait."

I was at the front counter going over Scorch's condition and dosage, when I saw the state police had pulled up outside. So I went out to make the report and show him the damage. He took the report, and I went back in to finish paying for Scorch's meds. When I walked in the door, the entire staff of the animal hospital was staring at me.

"Everywhere I go!" I wailed. "THEY FIND ME!"

Scorch opened his mouth wide, in a happy pant. He really seemed to be laughing.

That night, Scorch was lying flat out on his side, breathing his raspy, sick-dog breath and I sat down with him and explained it all. I said, "Now Scorch, you have been prayed over and energized and had hands laid on you and candles lit, and prayer chains and chemotherapy'd, and now you're getting magic potion too. I don't know how much more I can do. You have been great, through everything. But I am asking you for a few more days."

At this, he heaved a big, tired sigh.

I was not crying or allowing myself to be emotionally upset. I was downright cheerful.

I said, "I know right now you want to just quit. You would like to go see Reva, and Piper, and Bill the Cat (at this, his ears perked up) and George."

He lay still, staring straight ahead.

"That is fair enough," I added. "And if you give me these days, I promise at the end, if you still want to go, you can go. I will be okay with that. But you might only want to go because your body wants to. Maybe you will feel better. And if you feel better, you might want to stay with me. That would be great!"

He lay there patiently, listening.

"So, I am asking you to hang in there with me, just a few more days, to see if this magic potion works."

No reaction.

"It won't hurt!"

At this, his head came up suddenly. He looked straight at me.

"I'm telling you, it won't hurt at all! No needles, no chemo, no IVs. No poking. No blood samples. All it is, is just that stuff I squirted in your mouth, twice a day. That is all!"

He lay his head back down again.

"So. That's what we'll do, for a few days okay? And you might feel better because of the Pred. But we're going to just see. In the end, it's going to be up to you."

I got up off the floor then and went to the kitchen, and Scorch, who earlier had to struggle just to right himself, literally sprang to his feet. He went outside, trotting out to the bathroom area with Cajun. Then he came back in and had cookies and chicken. He even did a couple of tricks.

I had asked Scorch for a few more days, and that is exactly what he gave me. He gave me three days. On the third day, he was so weak that he didn't want to lift his head. He lay in a strange position on the living room rug, up on his sternum but with his head on its side; like how I would lay if I had a really bad migraine.

I had fought this for so many months, but seeing him like this, I couldn't get the vet out fast enough. We had to wait for an hour for Dr. Woody to show up. Kern Road's other vet, Dr. Linda Surch, loved Scorch and volunteered to come along too. But she got another call, and when Dr. Woody and technician Brenda showed up, she said, "Linda is sorry she couldn't come. She wanted to be here."

When he heard them arrive, Scorch got up to greet them like any good host would do. We went outside. Cajun came out carrying Scorch's new toy, a multicolored stuffed fleece ball. "Lie down," I told him, and he lay near the porch. "Stay there." He stayed there, holding the ball between his paws, and watching the proceedings.

Scorch crossed to the bathroom area, but he couldn't make it all the way there. He had diarrhea in the driveway. He turned around and came back. He went first to Dr. Woody, then to Brenda, and then when he got to me he collapsed in the grass at my feet.

I sat down with him, cradling his head in my arms. "Thanks for staying," I said. "You did great."

I was not going to cry until after he was gone. Dr. Woody settled near Scorch's back leg, and gently inserted the needle. "We love you so much, Scorch," she crooned.

Scorch lay in my arms, breathing his raspy breath, looking at me. Suddenly, his eyes popped open wide. He was looking up at something just past my head. It was so clear that I turned to look, too. There was nothing there. I turned back to him, and his eyes were half-closed again, and then he took his last breath.

I just sat there with him for awhile. I didn't want to let him go. I didn't want him to go.

I had decided to have him cremated, so I could keep him close to me always, which is where he always wanted to be. I had to send his body with Dr. Woody. When I finally was able to get up, I looked at Cajun and saw that he had pulled the stuffing out of Scorch's toy, and the white puffs were littering the yard. My dogs never did that. They were not allowed to destroy their toys.

"It's okay," I told him. "You can get up now."

He followed us as we lifted my beloved Scorch and laid him in the back of Dr. Woody's van. As they pulled away, I looked at Cajun and said, "We need to take a walk."

We drove down to the Lakeland Trail, where Cajun loved to go. As we pulled in to the parking area, on the ground was a colorful stuffed ball, exactly like the one of Scorch's, which Cajun had just torn up.

Chapter Five

It is easy to say how we love new friends, and what we think of them, but words can never trace out all the fibers that knit us to the old.
~ George Eliot

A message chimed in on my voice mail. It was my brother Dan. "Cowboys do not attend events like Cowboy Christmas. On a Saturday night, in Lansing, cowboys are at the Old Time Buckaroo's Saloon. They are line dancing with their bandannas, and their boots and their hats. You might even find one or two that has a lasso on 'em. So just a little heads up for you, there. You're looking in the wrong place for them there cowboys."

He turned out to be right. Cowboy Christmas was a horse show where I'd been invited to sell books and art. The Pavilion was decorated in garland and lights, and Andy Williams was singing merrily over the loudspeaker, but practically no one was there.

I had set up my booth, and I had a small tree with ornaments, a stack of Clifford books, and prints featuring my equine art. It was my second attempt to begin to recover from the emotional and financial devastation of losing Scorch. My first had been the

Novi Expo, where the North American Horse Spectacular was held annually in November.

The Expo was normally Clifford's gig. He loved greeting the thousands of people that showed up. He had been the Morgan ambassador for several years by that time. He loved showing off his tricks for an audience.

The 2005 Expo took place three weeks after Scorch died. That year I took Trudy, because she was the star of *Return to Manitou*, which I had published that year. I really wanted to promote the new book.

I think Clifford knew exactly where we were headed. He yelled furiously from his stall when I pulled Wheelzebub down the driveway.

Trudy wasn't cut out for the Expo. She was okay the first day, but after a twelve hour day on Saturday, she stood with her head in the corner like many of the other horses. To make matters worse, people were constantly coming up to me saying, "Where is Clifford? I want to see him play fetch."

Then, at the peak of the weekend, one of the Icelandic people came over to me. "Nancy, where is Scorch?"

I burst into tears. I clapped my hand over my mouth and forced myself to stop, so I could explain to the girl what had happened. "Oh no!" she said. "I'm so sorry! I will never forget all the tricks he used to do. And how he never left your side. He was just not like any other dog."

It was, overall, a pretty miserable weekend.

After Scorch died, sleep was my only refuge. I didn't want to get out of bed. Poor Cajun needed me, but sleep kept pulling me back. I wish that I could say that I was braver, stronger, more hopeful. But I just wanted to pull the covers over my head and hide from life; a life where cancer could take a dog who wasn't like any other dog. A life where six months of chemotherapy and thousands of dollars would not save him. A life without Scorch.

I was flooded with calls and emails. "Oh Nancy," Lori wrote. "I just want to lay my head down on my desk and start bawling."

Scorch had friends all over the world. It seemed everyone I had ever known, or talked to, and some I hadn't, was following his progress. I heard from people in Germany and Scotland and Australia. He had friends in Canada and all over the United States. Most of these, of course, were people who had only seen his picture, read about him in *Clifford of Drummond Island* and *Return to Manitou,* or were following his story through emails.

One day, I received a package in the mail from MSU. It was a children's book called, *Dog Heaven* by Cynthia Rylant. It was a wonderful, big book filled with vivid paintings of dogs frisking and playing in green fields under colorful skies. It was signed by every staff member who had treated Scorch. When the book arrived, I said to Cajun, "Look! We have to read this."

I sat down on the footstool and opened the book. "Come here."

Cajun came over and sat down. I started reading. "When dogs go to heaven, they don't need wings because God knows that dogs love running best."

Cajun started looking around.

"Pay attention!" I read on. "He gives them fields. Fields and fields and fields."

Cajun began to whine a little.

"Shut up and listen!" I turned the page. "When a dog first arrives in Heaven…"

Cajun yawned, a big, consuming, whistly yawn.

"Fine!" I shut the book. "Don't say I didn't try! But I want you to know, Scorch would have really appreciated this story! He would have hung on every word!"

Cajun gave me a sort of embarrassed look. He was right. There was really no comparing them. For Cajun's sake, I needed to get out of the house. I remembered the battered butterfly, and the deer I had hit with the car. I realized that like them, I needed to get up and keep moving.

Cowboy Christmas was slow. I think I sold two ornaments all evening. It started at 6 pm, so Caje and I got there about 4 to set up. As that evening wore on I started to think about leaving early, having so much to do at home. As is the wont of vendors everywhere, I wandered over to another booth to gab with other vendors. We were exchanging horse stories when a lady walked past with two Australian Shepherd pups, heading for the door.

Wait!" I said. "Don't go!" I ran after her. She obliged me and stood smiling while I got down to pet the puppies, a matched pair of tricolor females, about four months old.

The pups came right to me and let me hug them. There was no biting, no timidity, and they were so very cuddly, and of course, the next thing I knew, I was sobbing into their soft fur.

"I just lost my Aussie," I said to their owner. I couldn't go on. Who could explain a dog like Scorch? Those of us who grieve are like pieces of Swiss cheese, walking around with big holes in our centers, hoping no one notices, trying to be normal.

I tried to apologize but she said, "It's okay, we've all been there." She kindly added, "They're great therapy."

And they were! It was hard to feel sad with these two -- they were sort of mannerly, and so friendly. Their coats were clean and silky. I asked her where she had gotten them and she explained that a breeder had had "too many" and sold them "cheap". I took this to mean that they were sort of rescued. It was hard to believe that this would be a backyard breeder's efforts. The pups were, to my limited knowledge, very correct and they seemed very social. "I'll see if I can put you in touch with the breeder," the lady offered.

I had an ideal already in mind. I knew at some point Cajun and I needed another dog, but it was going to be a mutt, rather bizarre looking, some type of rescue, and preferably male. I knew that I was looking for Scorch, but not admitting it. I had already signed up with several rescue groups who were sending me options but I hadn't seen anything I needed.

I introduced myself to the lady, whose name was Jen. I wiped my eyes and told her I was a vendor and she politely came to look at my ornaments. She had heard of the Clifford book and we chatted while the puppies met Cajun. The smaller female shrank away from him at first. Jen said, "She belongs to my friend Sue. She is a bit soft."

Poppy, Jen's pup, charged up to Caje without fear. Cajun was overjoyed. They had a great time playing.

The more I talked to Jen, the more I learned we had in common. She had a big, German bred dog at home, that she had done some agility and protection work with, and had to keep busy. He sounded much like Cajun, except he was a Giant Schnauzer. Jen had horses too. I thought for sure she needed to be off somewhere, but she just kept hanging out and letting Cajun enjoy these puppies. The little one moved in a u-shape, trotting with her head down and rump rounded, very typically Aussie. She sort of floated, and her movement was liquid, rippling and effortless.

"She is really nice," I said.

Sue, the little one's owner, came up then. "I think she wants your dog," Jen said.

I just laughed. I was sure there was no way they would part with these pups and I hadn't even really considered that.

"She's already sold," Sue said. "There's a team penner who wants her."

"She's up for grabs?" I said in surprise.

"Yeah, I am moving -- I can't keep her. She just needed a home so I took her."

"You should let Nancy have her," Jen said. "She'd be a lot better home. Her other dog is in this Clifford book. He was in chemotherapy. And look at this German shepherd. He does agility and tracking."

She had been screening me, and I didn't even know it!

Sue came over and started looking at my book. "Would you be interested in this puppy?" she said.

I looked at the little one, the floating girl, and she

looked right back at me, her sweet expression framed with soft black feathers, and little brown peanuts over her eyes. "Who wouldn't want HER?"

"I'm gonna go talk to him," Sue said. She left. Jen wandered off with her. I went back to my vendor friends.

"I might get a puppy." I said. I was very casual, thinking it would not happen. This was a purebred dog, a female. Not a mutt, not a boy, and not bizarre looking at all.

The vendors said, "Really? One of those beautiful puppies?"

I shrugged. "If it is meant to be, it will be."

We talked for awhile, about fate, and I told them how this story of the puppies had just sort of unfolded, bit by bit. Then Sue walked up. She just looked at me, smiled and nodded.

I started hopping up and down. "She is mine? REALLY?"

She laughed. "Yes. I'll barter for her. You can paint my friend's dog."

I threw myself on this poor woman and hugged her. It just didn't seem real, that I would be able to have the puppy that easily. The world was expanding, wider, wider, and in the space of just about two hours, I had a puppy, and two new friends -- kind and generous people. And so, I thought, this is how things can happen in your life, a sudden splash when you least expect it, and then the world expands from there. It was like a stone thrown into a pond, and so the puppy was named Ripple.

Chapter Six

Communication is about being effective,
not always about being proper.
~ Bo Bennett

My brother Ted saved Christmas that year. He bought me a ticket to Tucson. This turned out to be a good idea. It was so different there, and far away. My new friend Jen kept Ripple and Cajun for me, and the neighbors looked after my horses.

Scorch had loved Christmas. He opened his own presents, wore a Santa suit and he had one special toy, a stuffed sleigh. It played a little jingly tune. He would play that thing over and over! If I had stayed home, I don't see how Christmas would have been bearable.

The desert was a good place to be. It was sunny and 70 degrees. We visited the Arizona Desert Museum and saw the raptor's free flight, and the art gallery. Ruthie's sister Debbie owned a horse, a palomino gelding named Poppin, and she took me riding. I couldn't imagine a nicer way to spend Christmas Eve.

Around that time, I decided that there was definitely something to this animal communication business. Debbie had an Akita mix named Gracie who gave me a clear picture of a black and white kitten. I knew Debbie had two cats and asked if one was black and white, and sure enough. That kitten was sucking on Debbie's neck at night. I had a strong feeling from Gracie about this kitten, but either was not experienced enough, or didn't trust myself enough to understand what it was. I began firing questions at Debbie, "Does Gracie like the kitten?"

"Oh yes."

"Has the kitten nursed on Gracie?"

"Yes, she used to, but Gracie won't let her do it anymore."

At that point I got the message. I said, "Debbie, if I tell you something about Gracie, will you promise not to think that I am crazy?"

Luckily for me, she was very open to this. So I told her, "Gracie thinks that it is ridiculous that the kitten is not weaned yet!"

Debbie started laughing. It turned out that when the kitten woke up at 3 am to suck on Debbie's neck, Gracie would poke her nose up on the bed. Debbie thought she was just jealous!

I was further able to ascertain that Gracie had hip dysplasia, but I did not want to tell Debbie that. So I told her that Gracie's hips were sore. I also picked up on the fact that Gracie thought the floor was hard. I asked if she slept on the cold floor next to a wall, and Debbie said yes, she slept in a hallway. I said, "She would like a rug there."

At this point Debbie started asking me what else Gracie had to say, but I just shook my head and said, "I don't know, I am too new at this."

Gracie probably had plenty more to say, but I just didn't want to be wrong.

When we went to Ruthie's mom's house, we were greeted by a beautiful brown and white Jack Russell terrier named Sam. When I crouched down to say hello to him, I tried to send him the message that I was in terrible pain and I was so happy that a dog lived here. From that point on, he became my constant shadow. "Sam likes you," Ruthie's mom said. "He could use a good trainer. If he came to live with you, you'd have him cooking your breakfast!"

Unfortunately on Christmas morning, Debbie and Ruthie's mom began a conversation about a dog Debbie had had to euthanize two years prior.

"She was just getting weaker and weaker. There was nothing I could do."

"They're getting snow back in Michigan," I said.

"She held on for as long as she could. I think she was waiting for me to arrive at the hospital."

The conversation had been going on for several minutes by this time and I could no longer speak.

"Then I walked in and she was lying on the exam table, but she just started wagging her tail," Debbie added.

That did it. I jumped up and went running into the bathroom, leaving Ruthie's family completely baffled. I sat down on the floor near the tub. I couldn't breathe, and my brother came to the door, and Sam rushed in, started jumping on me and licking my face. I looked up and was surrounded by faces, all worried, a couple of them starting to cry. I was trying to catch my breath. Sam was jumping on me urgently, and someone picked him up and took him away, but I wanted him to stay.

"I'm so sorry!" Debbie said. "I didn't know!"

Someone handed me a warm washcloth. I put it against my face. I could not speak. I was embarrassed, telling myself to calm down.

"It's okay," Ted said. He took my hand and helped me up. "You can cry if you want to."

"I can't." I said. "If I start, I will never stop. Too much will come out. Everyone will know there is something wrong with me."

"There's nothing wrong with you!" Ruthie's mom said. Now everyone was crying. Everyone except me.

I tried to apologize for ruining Christmas, but they wouldn't hear of it. There was nothing else to do but go on with festivities and try to salvage what was left. We did end the day with laughter.

Then, when I returned to Michigan, it was a whole new year.

Chapter Seven

All life is an experiment.
The more experiments you make the better.
~ Ralph Waldo Emerson

Clifford's knee was getting worse. It was big and lumpy, and I decided I had better have it checked. It was possible that surgery could help him.

We arrived at Kern Road Vet Clinic for his x ray to be faced by a very young, very unimpressed Dr. Christina Kobe. True to form, he did everything in his power to try to win her over, including nibbling and blowing on her. When that didn't work, he decided to shower her with a sneeze.

"Thank you very much. Just what I needed," she sighed. She was all business. She gave me a heavy lead vest to wear, donned one herself and had her assistant kneel next to Clifford's leg with a screen. She pointed the x ray machine at Clifford's knee, where it made a small red dot to mark the target area.

"You have to be still for a minute," I explained to Clifford. Despite his tendency to fidget, he stood with his head at my chest level, his ears at half mast, and waited patiently. When the shutter clicked, his head popped up as if he knew it was done. She took three pictures. During the last picture, she had her assistant hold Clifford's foot up so his knee could be caught in the bent position. He bore it all without moving.

"What a good patient!" Dr. Kobe murmured approvingly.

A few minutes later she came out with the films and put them up on the lighted screen, high on the wall. "Will he step over that cord so you can come and see these?" she asked, pointing at the electric cord on the floor.

"Sure." When we got over next to her, Clifford reached out and blew gently in her ear.

"You're very friendly," she said flatly. She pointed at the lighted images. The x ray revealed a bone chip floating in the inflamed tissue surrounding an arthritic joint. The spot where the chip broke away has an abrasive bone rubbing against the bone. "That foggy area is arthritis. That's what's causing his pain."

I asked her about arthroscopic surgery, and if it would help. "They could go in and remove the chip," she said, "But I don't think that's hurting him anyway. There's really nothing they can do for arthritis other than therapy. We can try bute to make him comfortable, and you can probably still use him for short rides. He's not an old horse, but at 15 he's no spring chicken, either."

I always wondered how much conversation Clifford understood, because at this he sort of flattened his ears and looked away.

"I'm on my way up to MSU today," she said. "If you like, I can take these x rays in, and see what they think."

"That would be great!" I said. "Let me give you my cell number."

The three of us walked over to a counter, and she took a pen that lay by the computer and wrote on Clifford's chart. Clifford stepped up to the keyboard and looked intently into the monitor. This last stunt worked, and Dr. Kobe finally burst out laughing. "Are you going to punch something in?"

"I think he wants to get on line," I said. Clifford rolled his eyes and nodded approval.

We headed home after that, where I researched bone chips in horses and found a horse named Be a Bono. He'd suffered a knee injury very similar to Clifford's. He was treated with his own stem cells, which they scooped from a spot near his tail and injected into his knee. He recovered and went back to the racetrack and won.

I finally got a referral to Dr. Caron up at MSU and emailed him:

Dear Dr. Caron,

Clifford, my Morgan, has bad arthritis in one knee, and a bone chip. He's got basically no cartilage left. He's 15.

I have heard great things about stem cell treatments for just this type of injury (specifically with a race horse called Be A Bono) and was wondering if you could tell me anything.

His response came less than ten minutes later:

Ms. Bailey,

We are not yet using stem cells for this purpose here, although it would not be that difficult to do so. I suspect that to compare your horse to Be A Bono might not be completely accurate - arthritis is a progressive disease and it sounds as if your horse has rather more severe disease. As such, results might not be all that you might anticipate. Nonetheless, I would be happy to examine your horse, discuss his past history and treatment and learn of your aspirations for him.

I immediately called the number and spoke to Carol the receptionist who said, "Are we talking about Clifford of Drummond Island?"

"Why, yes!" I said.

"My daughter has your books! She loves them!"

The morning of our appointment, Clifford knew something was up, and was not exactly cooperative. Usually not one to shirk an adventure, that day he was coy and difficult to catch.

"Come on Clifford, they are your fans and everything!" I tried coaxing him with grain and treats, but when he saw the halter coming at him he'd turn and bolt. One time he stepped on my foot. I finally stood next to his Dutch door and said, "Get in there!" and he walked in. I swung the door shut behind him. Once he was locked in the stall, he stood in resignation as I entered and put his halter on.

He loaded into Wheelzebub with no problem, and we were off, driving through the cold mist up to Lansing.

MSU's equine teaching hospital has wide hallways and big, roomy stalls, but to Clifford's chagrin, no shavings to roll in. My friend Rose appeared. Rose worked in the blood bank and she had helped take blood from Cajun, who had been a universal donor for several years. Rose emanated warmth. Animals loved her. She was petite, with a mass of dark curls sprawling down her back, eyelashes like fans, and a perpetual smile. She had the added appeal of being completely unaware of her stunning appearance. She went to Clifford immediately and said, "So this is the celebrity! Hello! Hi, it's nice to meet you!"

Other technicians gathered when they found out Clifford was fetching a cone in his stall. As soon as he had an audience, he visibly cheered up.

Dr. Caron was a tall, thin fellow with a somber demeanor, thinly disguising a sharp wit. As Rose and her gaggle of techies stood giggling and whispering around Clifford, he looked at me and said, "Do you want me to call security to come and get these guys out of here?"

We watched as he led Clifford out of the stall and trotted him up and down the generous hallways. Clifford was obliging enough.

"It looks like he's got a little muscle atrophy in that leg," Rose murmured. "It's thinner than the other."

"Really?" I squinted at Clifford but couldn't see the difference. The way he was moving seemed all right, but then the tech who led him did the flexion test, pulling his foot high so that his leg was bent sharply at the knee. She let go, and then when she asked Clifford to trot with her, he limped.

"We'll get some pictures of this and see how he looks," Dr. Caron offered. He turned and left the room.

Clifford went in for x rays and Rose and I hung out, drank coke, and talked about horses.

When Clifford's pictures were finally up on the lighted screen, I could see not one bone fragment but what looked like other chips floating in the same area. Dr. Caron looked on while Dr. Kimberly Roberts gave me the rundown. "His body is compensating for the arthritis, but I took a picture of his right leg so you can see how it's supposed to look."

Sure enough, the left knee by comparison was rough around the edges, all the way from front to back.

"He's not moving too badly," Dr. Caron said. "Are you riding him?"

"Not very much."

They went on to explain that, while they were not opposed to trying the stem cell treatments, and it might help him, they would suggest first attempting more conventional methods: Steroid injections and Bute.

"Well, I want to do things the right way," I said. I've never been a huge Bute fan because I've heard it's a temporary solution that can lead to overworking the horse and greater problems down the road. But, there is no cure for arthritis.

Had I been really adamant about it, they would have gone ahead with the stem cell treatments.

The stem cells would be removed from a spot near Clifford's tail, shipped to California where the cells would be isolated, then sent back and injected into his knee. The process would take a few days. They might help, or they might not make a difference.

"Would they do any harm?" I asked.

"No, other than you run the risk of infection in the injection areas," Dr. Caron said. "I'd like to see what stem cells would do for him, but I hate to use your horse as a guinea pig just to satisfy my scientific curiosity."

"Actually the guinea pig thing doesn't bother me, as long as it does him no harm... And especially if it benefits someone else."

I learned a couple more things about stem cells that I never knew: One, the injections would have to be repeated -- one would not provide permanent relief. The second thing was, in race horse Be A Bono's case, his injury was pretty fresh. Clifford's knee was fractured years ago. Stem cells may be more effective in a more recent injury.

There had been so little done with stem cells -- thanks to the expense -- that there was no way to predict how they would affect the patient.

So, in the interest of doing things the right way, I decided to follow their suggestion and try a less expensive and more conventional method -- steroids -- before I did any trail riding with Clifford that summer. Meanwhile, I'd continue to view stem cells as an alternative. I definitely hadn't ruled it out and in fact, was viewing this as a hoop I had to jump through to get there.

Chapter Eight

To help all created things,
that is the measure of all our responsibility;
to be helped by all,
that is the measure of our hope.
~ Gerald Vann

I was sitting on my friend Robert's back porch when I noticed a small dog peering at me through the fence. She was tied to a tree next door. The dog was white with brown and black spots. She was looking at me solemnly with dark brown eyes, but had one ear up and the other tipped over. This gave her a sort of crooked look and I had to laugh. I went over to the fence to speak to her and she began jumping straight up, chest high. I could see that she meant me to catch her, so I could untie her and help her over the fence.

"Sorry, I'm just petting you," I said. So she sat and gratefully allowed me to reach down and rub her crooked ears.

I learned that her name was Gem and she was tied to that tree most of the time. The rest of the time she spent in the sun porch, staring out through the window blinds she had shredded.

"Tell those people I want their dog," I said to Robert.

But later that day I saw a little toddler, a boy, hugging and kissing her, saying, "I love you, Gem," and that was the end of that.

Months went by and Gem continued her lonely life in the sun porch. Finally, one day that fall, Robert called me. "I have some good news for you."

"They left the dog!" I shrieked.

Sure enough, the neighbors had moved out and Gem was officially abandoned.

I brought her home and immediately began crate training. She was wild and unruly, and she had never been housebroken, having lived her life in that sun porch. But she bore everything with a good and honest nature. She was most cooperative with my dogs, and although mystified by my horses, didn't give them any trouble or get under their feet. She was smart, and clearly doing her best to fit in.

I took her to the MSU Small Animal Clinic, so she could get shots and a heartworm test, and to visit the blood bank so my friend Rose could see her. We sat talking with the door open. Rose had put a baby gate across the door so Gem wouldn't run out.

"What are you going to do with her?"

"I don't know. I can't explain it. The minute I saw this dog I knew I had to have her."

Just then a lady paused in the doorway, looking at us over the baby gate. "What a cute dog!"

"She's a rescue," Rose said.

Gem went straight to the woman, climbed up the baby gate and into her arms, and kissed her squarely on the lips. The lady's eyes began to well up. "Is she looking for a home?"

"Why?" I said.

"I don't know. I've just been praying that the right dog would come along. My Pomeranian is getting old, and I don't want my other dog to be alone. But I need one that will get along with my grandchildren and with horses."

I understood then, as sometimes happens in rescue, that I was like a relay runner, and Gem was the baton. The timing, in this case, was just right.

Chapter Nine

Always do your best.
What you plant now, you will harvest later.
~ Og Mandino

While walking the dogs I noticed something small and round lying on the dirt road in front of me. I picked it up. An onion.

It was harvest time and the big trucks were piled high with them, load after load of golden, peeling orbs. Now they were all over the road, scattered like apples, the air laden with their pungent scent. Some of them were split open revealing the smooth white surface inside, others had been flattened by tires. But most of them were firm and round.

I didn't have anything to put them in, or I would have squirreled some home. I decided to come back later with a bag.

So the day waned, shadows lengthened and I decided it was onion gathering time. I selected a plastic bag with handles, because I thought Clifford should help me get the onions. It would be a good little jaunt for him. I took the bag to the barn with me and a couple of apples. Clifford stuck his head eagerly in his halter, and I led him out and started to brush him.

A puff of air picked up the bag and moved it gently down the aisle toward his feet. He put his nose down and touched it.

Seeing him do this prompted an experiment, and I talk to him much as I would have done with Scorch. After all, he had been clicker trained the same way.

"Pick that up," I told him.

He lifted his head and looked at me. I used the same hand gesture that I had used with Scorch, pointing at the plastic bag and saying, "Pick it up."

I was not sure he knew what that meant. He had never been asked to pick up a bag, nor had he really been asked to pick up anything that wasn't first tossed by me. But he obediently bent down, picked up the plastic bag and put it politely in my hand.

"Good boy!" I squealed. I gave him an apple.

He crunched down his apple and then he wanted to make out. He stood with eyes half closed and kissed my shoulder and cheek, blowing on me softly. The only long term man in my life. Sigh.

I put the saddle and bridle on him. Cajun and Ripple were ecstatic at the prospect of a ride, and they darted around the yard panting eagerly. Clifford stood still while I got on, and we walked down the hill in the warm Indian summer, amidst the soft bird song and goldenrod in the slanted evening light.

There were fewer onions now, as many had been scavenged, but there were still dozens on the road. I dismounted and opened the plastic bag. Clifford's ears perked up and he immediately tried to grab the bag. I was bending over by the roadside with the reins in one hand and the bag in the other, attempting to pick up onions. But all Clifford wanted to do now was get that bag!

He bumped and jostled me in his fervor and nearly stepped on me. I was beginning to comprehend the err of my ways, because how could I in good conscience now discourage him from doing this?

Finally we edged to the roadside and his attention turned to the tall grass growing there. Great. Another bad habit. But I let him pull up grass. He got a mouthful and then walked along with me while I collected the onions.

At last, we had a bag full. I climbed back into the saddle and we started for home. I decided to shorten the trip because the bag was heavy, so we cut through the neighbor's field to go in the back way. I couldn't hold the bag by the handles for fear it would break. I hadn't thought about the weight of all these onions. So I rested it on the pommel ahead of me. The bag swished and crackled loudly with the motion of Clifford's shoulders as he walked, but obviously it didn't bother him.

We were almost back to the barn, when suddenly, the bag split. Onions began rolling down Clifford's sides, one after the other. Big ones. Small ones. They rolled down Clifford's shoulders, past his knees and thunked softly into the grass. He kept walking, turning his head this way and that. He cocked his left ear, then his right in corresponding direction to the falling onions. I was laughing so hard I couldn't hang on to them, and the bag was tearing more and more. Pretty soon they all had fallen.

It was a short distance, so I took Clifford home. He was happy now because he got to gallop a bit. As I ventured back out to the onions with a paper sack, Trudy stood with her head over the fence giving me an admonishing look. I was sure she knew that had I taken her instead, there would have been no such foolishness.

Chapter Ten

A sense of humor is a major defense
against minor troubles.
~ Mignon McLaughlin

Anne's trail ride was staged in a county park near Davison, Michigan, with plenty of wooded paths, fields, and late fall color. It was scheduled to be three hours long. That probably wasn't the smartest thing for me to do, because Clifford, besides having the arthritic knee, was fat and out of shape. The weather was pretty mild, in the sixties, amazing for this time of year. He jumped into Wheelzebub without hesitation and we hauled up to Anne's.

There were five of us, all aboard Morgans save for the one quarter horse. Clifford, with his big stride, started out in his customary place at the head of the pack. I decided to let him stay back a little because Anne was riding Blitz, her palomino Morgan stallion. Blitz had perfect manners, but why try to compete?

I could tell Clifford was not the same as in years past. He opted to go around mud holes now, and fallen trees, instead of over and through. He had lost a lot of flexion in the knee and couldn't step as high anymore.

But we still had a good time, laughing and chatting as we meandered along the winding trails through the blazing fall colors. A little breeze kicked up and dried leaves rained softly down on us.

Cajun and Ripple cavorted happily, swishing through the foliage. The horses didn't seem to mind, although Blitz kept looking at them and Anne thought he might want to race. Her mare, Jingles, was last in our troupe and she had fallen back a little. Finally I heard a voice, "Nancy, call Rip!"

I looked back, and Ripple was behind Jingles, busily nipping at her heels! She came away when I called her.

After a good hour and a half, we came to a water hazard. It was a canal at the bottom of a deep gorge, and was belly-deep on the horses. Clifford had been in water so much in his life, that I thought nothing of it. But as we splashed into the rushing current, I realized how cold it was. He climbed up the bank, and I was getting the idea that he was becoming uncomfortable. He didn't limp, but it was an idea, and after all these years together I could only surmise that it was right.

As we continued on, I realized Ripple wasn't with us and it occurred to me that she'd been in the water, but she'd never really had to swim. I called a couple of times, but she didn't come. Clifford turned immediately. He knew we had to go back for her. He tried to do his collected canter back to the gorge, but it felt stiff and wrong so I pulled him up. Just then, Ripple emerged from the ditch, completely drenched.

"You made it!" We turned and hurried back to join the others.

Anne's husband Rob met us at the clearing to take pictures. He graciously photographed each horse; the beautiful golden Blitz, the red bay mare Jingles, and then Clifford. I asked Clifford to stand by the chosen backdrop of oaks, and gave him the signal to stretch in a park stance. He had been trained to set his head, so that his neck arched like a classic Morgan. But as soon as he heard the shutter of Rob's camera, his head popped up. His ears thrust forward and his nostrils flared as he gazed at the camera. Everyone was cracking up! All training aside, it was just much more important to be a star.

Then we lined up for the group shot. The sorrel Quarter horse, the two bay mares, and Anne's palomino all posed nicely facing the camera, with Clifford and me on the end. Not satisfied with being one in a crowd, Clifford started to sink beneath me.

"ARE YOU CRAZY?" I shrieked, as he got lower and lower until finally he had flopped completely down on his belly. To my horror, Rob kept snapping photos as Clifford stretched comfortably out on his side, right next to where I was now sprawling on the ground.

He stretched his neck for a moment, snorting happily. Then apparently satisfied with the material he had provided, he got effortlessly back to his feet, and shook himself vigorously.

"Nice!" I told him. By now everyone was laughing again, and his expression was completely blissful.

I climbed back aboard. The photo session ended and we resumed our ride. Not long after this, I could feel how very stiff he was becoming. We were on a dirt road, but he still looked wistfully down every tree-lined path we went by. He loves the deep woods.

Finally he had begun to limp. I dismounted and we walked together.

"Do you want Rob to bring your trailer?" Anne asked. We agreed that was for the best, as there was still another half hour left to ride and we had to cross the water again. The nice lady on the quarter horse offered to let me double up, but I was content to just walk with Clifford.

I think if he had been in better condition, we would have been okay. I'd had a rough time adjusting to the thought of such a change, with him being only fifteen years old. But this ride had given me so much reassurance, because character-wise, he was still Clifford, after all.

Chapter Eleven

I believe cats to be spirits come to earth. A cat, I am
sure, could walk on a cloud without coming through.
~ Jules Verne

Miss Clairol was always a lady, and at age fifteen she had not changed. But I knew something was wrong, even though her sweet Somali purr had not subsided. A trip to the vet revealed a growth in her throat. I decided there would be no heroics, no surgeries. I brought her home with antibiotics and steroids.

She ate chicken and cuddled and purred, but she grew weaker. On the third day, when she refused food, and the purring stopped, I decided enough was enough. That morning I tried to put her in the carrier, and she struggled for the first time in her life. She didn't want to go anywhere. She wanted to stay home and die under my bed.

"It's okay," I told her. "Reva will be waiting for you."

Clairol was born with a blocked tear duct. This made her unable to nurse, since she had no sense of smell. I raised her on a bottle. Reva, my German shepherd, helped me nurse her. She would lie with the tiny kitten, nuzzling and licking her. She became Claire's surrogate mom. For the rest of her life, Claire had occasional trouble with upper respiratory infections. But she grew fat and happy and played just like any other cat. Reva watched over her, making sure the other dogs didn't bother her while she ate, and making sure that her face and nose was always clean. Reva seemed to understand exactly what Claire needed. The two were very close, sleeping together and sometimes even eating from the same bowl.

When Reva died in 2001, Claire shifted her adulation to Cajun. Maybe it was because he also was a German shepherd, but I suspect it was more due to his sweet nature. The two of them spent many long hours cuddling and kissing, and really were quite maudlin at times.

So, that morning on the way to the clinic, I explained to Claire where she was going. "You won't have any trouble breathing again, ever. And when you get there, you should just go straight to Reva. I know she will be waiting for you."

It was a great comfort to me, picturing Reva there to greet her, and part of our family being together again.

I brought Cajun into the clinic with me, so he could understand what was happening, and have a chance to say goodbye to his friend. Unfortunately, it was a struggle with Claire. She didn't want to lie on her side, because she couldn't breathe. The vet finally decided to put her under first with a simple shot under the skin. It took Claire about ten minutes to go to sleep. I put a little blanket on the floor for her, she went to sleep with her dog licking and cleaning her face.

Then, the vet and technician had trouble finding a vein. Poor Claire at four pounds was so frail that the doctor finally said, "She isn't breathing. She technically is gone, but her heart's still beating. I'm going to have to put the shot into her heart."

It's not like this wasn't traumatic enough. I found an excuse to leave the room by taking Cajun back to the car. He gave one final lick to Claire's tail, which was hanging off the edge of the table, and then followed me out.

I had some guilt about missing Claire's last moments, even though I knew she didn't know anything. I still needed to collect her body, which they were putting in a box for me. So I came back into the clinic. A red and white cattle dog greeted me enthusiastically in the lobby. I spoke to it as I went by. Then someone called my name.

I turned, and to my surprise, I saw my friend Kelli holding the cattle dog's leash. Seven or eight years prior, Kelli had been my pet sitter. She was familiar with my whole clan. We hugged, and I burst into tears, "I just lost Miss Clairol."

"Oh no! I'm so sorry!" She kept hugging me and hugging me. The cattle dog was nudging my leg, and I bent to pet her. She thrust her nose into my hand and licked it eagerly.

Kelli said, "This is Reva."

I was too stunned to react at first. It was implicit that Kelli's Reva was named after mine. In fact, Kelli was almost apologetic about it, as if she had stolen the name! "It just seemed to fit her."

The dog was very urgently trying to keep my attention the whole time. Finally, Kelli asked, "Do you still have Reva?"

I smiled through the tears. "No, Reva died in 2001. But she is clearly still with us."

I could see that Kelli immediately knew what I was saying. She hugged me about four more times. The Cattle Dog Reva kept watching to make sure I absolutely got the message.

From that moment on, I felt at peace for Claire. I knew that someone had been listening, and that she was in a very safe place.

Chapter Twelve

Action is the real measure of intelligence.
~Napoleon Hill

Ironically, I was investigating the subject of horse intelligence, when something happened in the barn. Clifford, who often lets himself out of the stall if I leave the door unlatched, did so that day. I was busy with the water bucket, and didn't really mind. He often wanders loose around the backyard. There was a blizzard that day, though, and the snow was really piling up outside. Since I was down at the end of the aisle, I couldn't do much about it when I heard Trudy's hoof beats clopping across the rubber mat on Clifford's floor. She had walked in through his open Dutch door, and then let herself out into the barn aisle. She took off out the door after him.

Two loose horses can geek each other up pretty easily, especially when the weather's cold. These two snorted and took off, bulldozing through the drifts, lifting knees and hocks high. Cajun and Ripple, squealing with excitement, bolted after them. In two seconds dogs and horses were gone over the hill in front of the house.

I called the dogs back. They reluctantly allowed me to shut them into the feed room.

Quelling my rising thoughts about how slippery the roads were, I knew that to remain calm was the most important thing. I couldn't see up over the hill, but hoped they hadn't gone far. If I went after them, it would probably have the same effect as the dogs chasing them. I went into the feed room and filled the scoop with grain.

I did feel lucky that it was dinner time, but I had spent so many hours with these horses at liberty that I wasn't overly concerned. Clifford was seventeen that year; having lived with me and having lots of freedom for fifteen years. Trudy was fifteen, and she's been with me for twelve years. They had both run loose on the beach up on Drummond Island, and for their entire lives, had been treated more like big dogs than livestock.

As a dog trainer, I had found Clifford to be almost prodigiously smart. His antics had led to the book about him. I had **blogged** about an incident with Clifford from just two days prior. It was very cold that day. The horses were so happy! They weren't even as voracious for their hay as I imagined they would be. I had left a few carrots in a bag in the barn and in the cold weather they had frozen. I dropped one as I went into Clifford's stall. Since I had a bucket in my other hand, he was focused on that and didn't notice the carrot on the floor.

"I dropped a carrot," I said to him. I pointed at it. "It's right there. Pick it up."

He immediately left the bucket chase to follow the direction of my pointing finger and get the carrot.

Sure, he was clicker trained, and could fetch a cone and other stuff, but this showed me that he had a complete understanding of the whole "point and fetch" concept -- because he hadn't known the carrot was there. Furthermore, to walk away from a known food source – the bucket – to follow my empty hand gesture meant he had a good understanding of what was in store. I was pretty flabbergasted.

This led me to search online for some details about a horse's cognitive abilities. It appeared that there hadn't been much research done.

I did learn that one of the best known researchers working on cognition specifically in horses was Evelyn Hanngi, PhD. She was president of the **Equine Research Foundation** in Santa Cruz, California. She had done some simple experiments in an attempt to learn whether a horse can apply concepts.

The horse is shown a panel depicting two images -- one of an open circle and one of a filled circle. If the horse touches the open circle it gets a treat. If it touches the filled circle, nothing happens. I can say pretty certainly that if Clifford were faced with this choice, the filled circle wouldn't stand a chance. He would have it in about two minutes. Dr. Hanngi's horse did too.

Dr. Hanngi went on to get her horse to differentiate between other shapes as well. There might be an open and a filled square or an open and a filled triangle. The horse figured them out.

One could argue that my episode with Clifford and the carrot could have been a "Clever Hans" type of reaction -- my body lingo cueing him for the correct response. But those of us with horses know that they are smart, and it could be kind of silly to try to quantify the obvious. It's like scientists suddenly discovering that pets have emotions.

As for my two escapees, well, I stood in the doorway with my scoop of grain and called their names. They came plunging back down the hill through the snow, knocking sheets of it high around them. That wasn't good enough, though. They had to make a couple of circles around the house before they finally deigned to come back in, snorting, wild-eyed and each carrying a white blanket on their backs.

As I watched them prancing toward me, it occurred to me that it wasn't surprising that their intelligence had not been measured. Their beauty is so distracting; their abilities so all-encompassing; their history so fascinating. There are just so many other things to learn about the horse.

Chapter Thirteen

The secret of health for both mind and body is not to mourn for the past, nor to worry about the future, but to live the present moment wisely and earnestly.

~Buddha

I didn't take the horses back to Drummond during those following years. It was too painful with Scorch being gone, and I had heard that they were starting to tear up the trees around Clifford's Bay. I couldn't bear it.

I took Clifford out for short rides around the farm. It was spring. The red winged blackbirds serenaded us as we clopped up the road.

Clifford was happy to go; in fact he stopped me from taking his halter off. He mashed his lips against mine and stood there for a long time, gently flipping his upper lip. He had a glazed over look. I half expected him to slip me the tongue.

Finally I convinced him it was time to quit kissing and get the bridle on. I kept a loose rein, allowing him to drop his head and plod along. He did not have the usual spring in his step, but wasn't limping either.

We went a couple of miles down the road and then came back. As we approached home, he got a little frisky and wanted to pick up the pace. I let him trot a little, and then he slowed to a canter. I wondered if a canter is easier, less jarring on the knee.

His knee didn't seem to be bothering him much. I alternated hand walking him with little rides. I enjoyed the walks just as much, although I think the dogs preferred the faster pace. I had a call from my friend, longtime Morgan trainer Sandy Crechiolo, who gave me lots of encouragement and referred me to a local vet that she said was very good with joints.

I was trying Clifford on a new product; a stem cell supplement. I wanted to give it 30 days and just see what happened. I took him off a glucosamine supplement so I wouldn't confuse myself about what was working. I wanted to wait and see how it worked before I say anything or recommend it.

Lately it had been pretty disheartening to see him hanging back when he saw me get the halter out. He was only seventeen and didn't want to work. But today he was more like his old self.

On day 6, we walked down the road with the dogs. On past occasions he had started to limp on the way back, so I'd opted to take a shortcut home. Today, he clopped along happily with me looking around at all the budding leaves. A couple of four wheelers drove past us. He'd seen those things so many times it didn't faze him at all, of course. We reached the corner where we normally turned around, and came back.

It was clouding over and a cool little breeze was kicking up. As we turned down the long driveway, those four wheelers came buzzing back up the road. Clifford sprang straight up and did an about-face in mid-air, landing in the opposite direction to face them, while I still held the lead rope.

This is one of his classic tricks and he was just playing a game, pretending to be "ascairt". But he had not performed this stunt in a couple of years. My laughter had always tended to egg him on, and now he began doing a piaffe beside me, blowing and snorting, eyes all ringed in white. We got to the base of the hill with him still prancing and arching his neck.

"Okay," I said. "I'm gonna let you go. Ready?"

I unhooked the halter and he took off, blasting up that hill with his tail held high and the dogs in hot pursuit.

I ran behind him swinging the lead rope and he did a beautiful extended trot all around the back yard, his tail flagging, in that floating gait I hadn't seen in so long.

I didn't know if this was due to the increased exercise, increased sweet grain (to mix with the new supplement) or the warmer weather. Or maybe he was just having a really good day. I was staying cautiously optimistic about the supplement, but it was really neat to see him jumping, bucking and playing with the dogs like he used to do.

Chapter Fourteen

Since there is nothing so well worth having as friends,
never lose a chance to make them.
~ Francesco Guicciardini

There was a glorious sunny sky in Michigan even though the breeze was bitterly hanging on to that whole winter idea.

I saddled up Clifford, and the dogs raced ahead joyously as we took a slog down the road. I use the word, "slog" not only because of the mud, but because that was pretty much Clifford's attitude. I thought his knee might be a little stiff. We got to the corner, which was only about a mile, and I started to turn him back.

Just then, the neighbor's German shepherd came bounding out, barking stiff-legged with his hackles up. Through the trees I could see a woman walking toward us. The dog bounced at her aggressively and she hesitated. She stood perfectly still as the dog took a couple more hops and stood a few feet from her, barking a loud warning.

I called the dog Cujo. I knew he lacked confidence, hence the behavior. He was scaring this woman and he knew it. But I was also privy to the fact that the owner had been doing bite work with him with a local K9 officer, and I didn't know if this meant that now the insecure dog thought he had permission to bite.

I sat quietly on Clifford watching this poor woman. I was in a bit of a quandary. Cajun was staying with me and Clifford. But if I approached that dog on the horse and he didn't back off, it would surely give Cajun incentive to give Cujo a good old fashioned whuppin'. If, on the other hand, Cujo went after this lady in earnest, I could send Cajun to the rescue. But Cajun loved to bite, and if he was given permission to do that, he might seriously hurt the dog. So I waited.

A second later Cujo noticed us watching, and dropped his tail and ran home. The lady came around the corner and gave me a nervous smile. As she walked toward us, this gave Cujo incentive to pursue her and now he stood at the corner barking at us all ferociously.

"He's pretty scary, isn't he?" I said.

"Yes, he sure is!"

I decided it was time to get off the horse, tell Cajun to stay, and chase that dog home. I held the rein out to the lady. "Would you mind holding him for a second?"

She backed away quickly. "Oh, I'm deathly afraid of horses."

"Oh, you are? All right." I sat up. "Well, let's just turn around and head back then."

I really didn't want to reward this dog's bad behavior by leaving. I especially didn't want him coming after us, because there was only so much of this that Cajun was going to tolerate. But I had no other choice. I turned Clifford around and we walked slowly away. Fortunately, we got off easily because Cujo did not follow.

The lady said her name was Connie and she lived down the road a piece. "I have to go back that way," she added.

"We'll walk you back," I said.

Connie was hitting a pretty nice stride that evenly matched Clifford's. I kept him on the right shoulder of the dirt road, and she stayed on the left. We talked pleasantly as we walked along. She said she had quit smoking in January, and was now trying to exercise more by walking every day.

"How long were you a smoker?"

"Twenty years."

"Wow! Good for you!"

Between this and the way she had faced that big scary dog, and now was walking the road with a scary horse, I could see that Connie had moxie. I liked her right away.

We headed along the road and looked at the farmer's fields, and talked about neighbors we knew, and how the land had changed over the past years. Connie was taking a pretty long walk. She wanted to go to the end, which was two miles away.

A car approached us from behind. "Car coming," I said to the dogs, and they quickly flocked to Clifford's side. The car passed slowly between Connie and us.

"Those dogs are really good," she said.

"Most of the time," I agreed.

Clifford had not been this direction in a long time. We don't usually go that way because the dirt hits pavement and then there's nowhere else to go. This was interesting for him. His ears were up and he looked around. He probably liked having the company too, because his stride lengthened and pretty soon he started to feel like his old energetic self.

I talked about Clifford and told Connie stories of his tricks, and the books, and told her about Morgan horses and how funny they are. We finally reached the road's end and then turned back. The chilling breeze cut into us as we headed back. Since now we were going homeward, Clifford's walk was even more vigorous. Connie was picking up the pace too.

"Is this too fast for you?" I said.

"No, this is good. But I see he likes to go faster up the hills!"

Another car approached, and this time, Connie moved over behind Clifford to let it pass.

The road stretched ahead, and as we passed our driveway, Clifford stepped irritably sideways. He was nearly bumping into our new friend in his effort to convince me to head homeward.

"Stop it!" Then I added, "That's our driveway. He thinks he needs to go back there and have supper. He thinks I'm starving him."

We walked up the little hill toward the corner, and as we topped it, I saw a herd of eight or nine deer bounding across the road in front of us, in full flight mode with tails up. Then, I saw why. Cujo was in hot pursuit, stretched out flat and running after them.

"Well, I guess we won't have to worry about him for awhile," I said.

We rounded the corner anyway and escorted her up the hill until she was safely past the house. Then we stopped to say goodbye.

"That was a great walk!" I said.

"Yes it was! Come again sometime. I'm going every day with my husband and we'll have a group sometimes."

"I might have a business card here," I reached into my pocket and found one. I held it out to her, and she stepped right up without hesitation and took it. She even stood by Clifford for a moment, although she didn't touch him. To my surprise, he was a gentleman and didn't attempt to sniff, kiss, rub, nibble or otherwise mug her.

As we parted ways, I called back to her. "That was very brave of you!"

"Well, I've been walking with him for awhile!"

112

she said.

At the corner, Cujo was still nowhere in sight. Clifford snorted happily as we headed for home.

Chapter Fifteen

Old friends pass away, new friends appear.
It is just like the days.
An old day passes, a new day arrives.
The important thing is to make it meaningful:
a meaningful friend - or a meaningful day.
~Dalai Lama

In the spring of 2008, I came home one day to find Cajun dead. He was lying in the dog pen, stretched out, mouth open, with an agonized expression.

It was too horrible for words. Cajun, like Scorch, was only nine years old. He looked and acted like he was five. When I went to open the gate, Ripple blasted out at me, leaping on me, very anxious. She had been with him through it. I held her for a minute, then went in to kneel beside the body of my longtime friend. I ran my hands over him. He was cold and stiff.

It was the third year after Scorch's death and I still had not recovered financially. I could not afford a necropsy on Cajun. It would not have helped him anyway. But I knew he had died of a blocked intestine, because I had given him a pork hide bone several days prior. The bone was supposed to be completely digestible. But he'd never had one before, and it was the only thing I could think of that I had done differently. Just the day prior, he had gone with me for a bike ride, and the day before that, he had walked with Clifford.

I called my brother, Dan, immediately, who lived three hours away in Cadillac. He agreed to drive down.

I was in shock. It seemed like a bad dream. I blamed myself. Why did I give him that rawhide? For months afterward, every time I had a stomach ache, I would cry and think about how he must have suffered. It was a horrible way to lose this wonderful friend.

He was buried under the pear tree, next to his beloved kitty, Miss Clairol. Cajun was a force, and his departure left a huge hole in many ways. It was my first time in over twenty years without a German shepherd in my life.

Ripple had been with him at the end, for which I was glad. I was already thinking of her as, "The Sympathy Dog." If I wept, she would come and try to press her lips against mine. If she even heard me sniffle, she would look up suddenly from across the room, trying to determine whether she should come over for a hug. I hadn't taken her to classes or taught her many tricks. Her job was simply to be there, and she did it well.

I was scheduled to ride Clifford in the Pinckney Memorial Day Parade the following Monday. I debated whether I should go or not.

Clifford was supposed to help my friend Dianne introduce her boyfriend's Tennessee Walker, Dollar, to the excitement of a parade. It was Dollar's first time in a parade. Since we were needed, I decided to go, knowing it would be good for me.

Dollar was escorted by Cliffy and me on one side, and Dianne and her horse Kinkaid, also a parade veteran, on the other.

It was a lovely day. Clifford was thrilled! We enjoyed an hour trail ride through Pinckney Recreation Area to reach the starting point at the school. When the parade was over, we took off for the trails again. Clifford was doing a lot of trotting to keep up with a batch of Walkers and I started worrying about his knee. I asked Dianne if she would mind separating from the group and just going back slowly with us.

"Sure!" she said. "I'll even ride behind you and let him set the pace."

We let the group go on without us. We turned up a trail through the woods. As soon as we got into the thick brush under the trees, I felt Clifford bunch up underneath me.

"He always wants to run in the woods," I called back to Dianne. Clifford was so eager to go that I finally just gave up and let him take off. WHOOSH! The next thing I knew, we were galloping up that path with the wind rushing through my hair.

"Good grief!" I shrieked as he hurled himself around a bend. I ducked easily under low hanging branches as Clifford charged ahead.

"Take a right up here!" I heard Dianne yell, but Clifford needed no direction as he veered to the right at the fork in the trail and blasted up another hill.

"Left!" Dianne hollered and again, Clifford chose the correct direction at the next fork. I could feel his power and it was just like the years had fallen away from us, reminiscing about speedy rides up on Drummond Island.

"I'm just going to quit calling directions and see what he does," Dianne said. I gave Clifford free rein and he correctly navigated the miles back to the farm where we started out -- all at top speed.

He was sweaty and blowing when we got back, but so happy. And -- he hadn't limped a step.

Chapter Sixteen

I heard my brother's voice even though we were apart.
~Maurice Gibb

Spring of 2008 marked a huge career change for me. It was every writer's dream. I was working with an agent, and I was able to connect with a wildlife rehabber from Seattle who wanted to tell his story about a totem bird that he had raised from a baby. He felt the bird had helped him through cancer treatment and into remission.

The story called to me in many ways, partly because of my experience with Scorch, and partly because of my love for wildlife. I loved the concept of the spirit of totem animals. I was so excited that I was chosen to write it. I introduced him to an agent that I had worked with. She was young and had a few "back shelf" sales under her belt. She had been unsuccessful in pitching the Clifford books and a couple of my other projects, but I liked her and thought she deserved a break.

I hit it off with Jim, the rehabber, and liked him tremendously. We seemed to have a good meeting of the minds. As my agent pitched the story, we were interviewed by a number of publishers, including, of all things, Harlequin. They were attempting to develop their mainstream line, outside of the romance novels.

The three of us spent over an hour on the phone one day with an editor from Harlequin. Jim said to me afterward, "I was surprised she spent so much time with us. I was going to ask you about the money thing. Seems to me they want a lot from you with no dough. You have to eat too."

I said, "I don't mind writing the chapters, as they have to be done, anyway. If Harlequin wants us, we can work our tails off and spank out a big book and maybe they will publish in spring of next year!"

"Hey, if they pay, I'm good with it. I have a question for you. How did you develop as a writer? Did you go to school, or…? I love your style. It puts me in the story."

"Thanks! I took some classes but it's mostly doing what comes naturally. In high school, my short story was a finalist in a national competition with something like 6,000 entries. It was sponsored by the Interlochen Arts Academy here in Michigan. They tried to recruit me as a student, but there wasn't any money to send me there. Kinda too bad, as I am sure I'd be farther along by now. Oh well."

"You would be huge and have no time for me."

"Nah, I'd have the same vision and you'd make me even bigger! Well, you and all the ice cream."

"It's hot here today; almost seventy. I need ice cream. That's the one thing I am addicted to and that I really have to watch how much I eat. I don't want to swell up like a pig."

"That's not why you're going to swell up. When this book comes out, it will be the women. You'll have marriage proposals. Indecent proposals. Lurid proposals. You'll have single women, married women, fat women, skinny women, homely women and pretty women all coming on to you. Your head will swell up so big that we'll have to get cables to hold you down, just like a float in the Macy's Thanksgiving Day Parade."

"I can get the cables. Are you looking forward to your trip? Lisa is cleaning the house so it will be nice when you get here."

"Yes, I can't wait! Tell Lisa not to worry too much, or I won't feel at home."

"Don't worry. After she's done I'll go up in your room and throw cat poop and dirt all around for you."

"Gee thanks."

"You're welcome. I'll be sure to hide the poop, too, so you can smell it but not find it."

"Nice. The host with the most."

Our conversations tended to evolve that way. We'd start out working on the book and then meander off into other areas. We laughed our heads off and teased each other constantly. I adored Jim. When we met on his doorstep, I ran straight to him, and he gathered me up for a big hug. My sister-in-law Judy, who was with me, said it looked as if we had known each other all our lives.

He was anxious to introduce me to the bird and said I could hold her if she would let me.

When I first saw the bird, she was in her flight waiting for Jim to come and get her. As I watched, she waddled across the ground, tried to step up on a limb, and lost her balance and tumbled off. She rolled over, stood up, and more carefully climbed up the limb. My heart went out to her. I admired her pluck and spirit.

It was a convenient visit for me, since my older brother Jon lived in Ellensburg, Washington, about ninety minutes from Seattle. I had flown all the way to Seattle from Michigan. It was spring in the mountains, and the lush green scenery was a healing sight for me. I was nursing a broken heart. Cajun had died just ten days earlier.

Jim found a glove for me, and he carried the bird as we walked down into a small grassy clearing. "We'll see what she does," he said. "She doesn't go to everyone, so don't take it personally if she refuses to step on."

The bird sat quietly on his arm, looking around. He handed me a long leather strap, similar to a dog's leash, and said, "Here, just hold this between your fingers. I'll keep the end of it."

I pulled the glove on and held my arm up in front of the bird's feet. Without hesitation, she climbed on board, and I was now standing with twelve pounds of eagle on my arm. I propped my elbow on my hip bone to manage the weight, and her head hovered just above my face. She sat there, seemingly content.

Jim smiled. "She likes you!"

He backed away from us a few feet, and let us commune. He still held the end of the leash, but it was loose, draping toward the ground. He wasn't worried. I spoke to the bird softly.

Jim said, "Hey, if she'll let you, just bury your nose in her chest and see what she smells like."

I did, inhaling the wonderful clean feather smell. I looked up, smiling. "She smells great!"

His expression was bemused, even amazed. "You are the only person besides me who has ever done that."

"Really?" I was truly honored. But I felt very comfortable with this big bird, in fact a sort of warmth emanated from her that was unique. I had held plenty of birds in the past, but I'd been around parrots that I wouldn't put my face this close to. For some reason, the trust between us was immediate and complete.

Then I started thinking about how special a friend she was to Jim, and how they had been together for many years. The inevitable happened. I thought of Cajun, my friend who would have been ten years old that summer. It was too much for me. Standing there under the trees, with that eagle on my arm, I began to weep. I stood there, crying softly, turning my face into her feathers. The bird snuggled up closer, hugging me with her body. She wrapped her right wing, the good one, around my back. I had the undeniable feeling that she understood. I felt her beak pulling softly at little strands of hair on my head.

Jim did not interrupt us. I felt as though she would have stayed there all day and comforted me if I needed it. Finally, after about twenty minutes, I thought I had monopolized her long enough and so I reluctantly gave her back. Before Jim took her, she reached out and tweaked my nose playfully. It was almost as if she couldn't resist the urge to try to make me laugh.

That alone would have been enough to sell me on the idea of totem animals. But later that summer something even bigger happened.

I was scheduled to fly back to Seattle to attend the powwow where the bird was to make the grand entrance. The day before my flight, I got a call from Judy, my brother Jon's wife. "Jon's been airlifted to the hospital."

"What?"

"He's really sick."

"What's wrong with him?"

"They don't know. He's coughing up blood."

Judy met me at Sea-Tac airport the next day. We went to the hospital together, to find my brother in an induced coma with a tube down his throat. Jon was in his late fifties, a big, strong outdoorsman who could walk miles in the mountains and seemed to be able to track an elk by scent alone. He had a boisterous and jolly nature. It was so odd seeing his large, powerful form lying with tubes coming out of him, breathing on a machine. He was bleeding into his lungs, and the doctors couldn't figure out why. While we stood staring at Jon, we overheard a doctor in the hallway referring to his case as, "interesting".

A week went by, and his condition remained the same. The doctors were conducting all kinds of tests. The family started showing up from all over the country: My elderly parents, two sisters and a brother came from Michigan, a sister from Colorado. We had plenty of questions, but no answers. No one was sleeping. We had dinner together, in a large group, laughing and telling stories about Jon. Now and then one of us would break off to go cry somewhere, or sit alone staring out the window. It was like a week-long memorial service, only Jon was still alive. It was the kind of nightmare that no family wants to go through.

I hated to tear myself away from the hospital to attend the powwow, but I thought I had better do it. I needed to experience it so that I could write about it. It was, after all, the reason why I had arranged the trip.

Somehow, even though she was reluctant to leave Jon's side, I managed to drag Judy along with me that day. The powwow was held in a big, green valley surrounded by trees. Crowds of people gathered around various vendor displays and snack wagons. Jim greeted us happily at the rescue group's tent. My friend the bird was there, inside the tent, resting on her perch and taking a break from the crowds.

"I'm so glad you made it!" Jim said. "How is your brother?"

I shook my head. "He's not good. It's his lungs. They keep filling up with blood. He can't breathe on his own."

Judy's expression was grim. I put my arm around her shoulder. We walked across the park, looking at all the Natives in their colorful regalia. We passed art booths featuring all kinds of animal figurines, wood carvings and feathers hung on dream catchers.

"I want to find something to take to Jon," I said. "Something that will bring him luck."

"Hmm," Jim said. "Well, there should be something here."

"His totem is an elk. What is the best thing for someone with an elk totem, who has an illness?"

"I don't know. Let me ask around."

Jim went back to the rescue booth and spoke with another one of the rehabbers. He came back a few minutes later. "She doesn't know. She thought maybe some kind of musk, but she doesn't want to be wrong."

I looked around. "I am sure there must be something. We'll keep looking."

"I know who I can ask," Jim said. He disappeared.

Judy and I kept moving, looking at handmade drums and leather goods. About ten minutes later, Jim came back. "I have something." He held out his fist. "Who should I give this to?"

"Give it to Judy," I said.

Judy held out her hand, and Jeff placed a small, ivory-colored object into it. "What is this?" Judy said.

"A whistle tooth," Jim said. "It's the first thing they told me, 'Whistle tooth'. I asked some folks I know, and they took me to this lady. She was in full regalia, and she took this right off her clothing and gave it to me. It's the tooth that the elk blows air through, when he bugles."

Judy and I looked at each other. Our mouths dropped open. "Judy!" I whispered. "It's the tooth the *air goes through*!"

Both of our eyes began to tear up, and we clutched each other briefly. We were standing right by a booth that sold leather, and we picked out a pouch – one that wasn't too girly – to put the tooth in. That night, we went back to the hospital and Judy hung the pouch on Jon's bed right by his left hand.

I met Dad in the hallway. My heart went out to him. The past weeks had taken their toll, and he was exhausted. He had suffered a small stroke the year prior. He looked the same, but his speech had been affected. He had to concentrate on his pronunciation when he spoke, and when he was tired, he slurred his words. He came up and kissed me briefly. "Hey," he said. "This morning I saw a bald eagle sitting on the church steeple! It sat there for the longest time."

Judy and I looked at each other again.

"Dad," I said. "Jon is going to walk out of this."

Dad turned and looked at me. His expression clearly said, "You're crazy," but he made himself smile.

Not long after that, doctors finally had a diagnosis. Jon had Microscopic Polyangiitis, a type of vasculitis affecting only three in one million people. Jon was on the ventilator for a month. When he woke up, he was so weak that he had to learn to walk all over again.

He was moved to a rehab center in Yakima, where he began physical therapy. Less than two weeks after that, he hobbled out to his car, climbed in, and drove himself home.

Today he and Judy are living in Ellensburg. Come spring, he'll be back in the mountains, tracking elk.

Chapter Seventeen

Bad times have a scientific value.
These are occasions a good learner would not miss.
~Ralph Waldo Emerson

In October, we sold Jim's story to a major publisher for a five figure advance. Our pitch had worked, and it looked like the book was going to be huge. We were really rolling.

I went into Clifford's stall, leaned my forehead into his white blazed face, and said, "It's going to be okay. We're gonna make it."

One big worry was resolved with this. Amanda had presented it to me earlier that year in her own blunt way. "I always thought, when Mom and Dad were gone, you would take care of me. You can barely take care of yourself!"

With a bestselling book, I was going to be able to take care of my parents. I was going to be able to take care of Amanda. I was going to keep rescuing animals. And the thing I could barely dare to hope for, my dearest dream, my greatest wish, was that I could save Clifford's Bay. I wanted to buy the property that was slated for development, and then donate it to the Nature Conservancy.

Work on the story commenced. But it wasn't easy. The editor didn't like the way I was writing it. She didn't have one positive thing to say about my style. She didn't like the fact that I was mentioning lice and feces, and other real life problems that occur with wildlife rehabilitation. She went to Jim secretly and offered him another writer. He said no, he was committed to working with me, and we had a good portion of the book completed.

My agent was nearly as bad when it came to the subject of Native American lore. She didn't know what "counting coup" was.

This was all okay, because I knew Jim got it, and we were on the same page. We talked every day. He had a good sense of humor and we were often immersed in bouts of hysterical laughter.

"I'm looking for other ways to exploit you," I teased. "Jim and the Bird action figures. Jim and the Bird claymation series. Jim and the Bird toilet paper."

"Keep thinkin, Sparky," he said. "That's what you do best."

I used my 401k, left over from my marriage, to live on while I wrote his story, to make the two trips out west to meet him and the bird. I never asked him for any reimbursement. I knew that if I put my whole heart into this, my effort would be honored.

Then, in November I got a call from my agent. "I have to talk to you. There is something wrong with the manuscript. The editor found plagiarism."

I was startled, but remained quiet for a minute, running the chapters through my head. I had been doing research on the internet, and probably had not edited some of it well enough. "Well, there may be a couple of spots I have overlooked. I will check them again."

"I knew it was a mistake," the agent said. "There's a fine line between research and plagiarism. Frankly, I'd take one of you over ten of some of these other authors."

That made my day!

I went back and looked at the emailed copy I had sent, thinking it was no big deal, but an unpleasant surprise awaited me. I had sent the editor the wrong draft of the chapter. Instead of deleting the old file, I had emailed it to her. In that early version, there was a paragraph where I hadn't cited my source, and I had not finished reworking it. She had noticed it immediately. I called the editor right away, and she started screaming at me. "You had to know! This isn't high school."

I was surprised at her behavior, but I apologized and then sent everyone an email assuring them it wouldn't happen again. Jim said, "Nancy, I believe in you. We'll be fine."

For the next two months, all through the Christmas holiday season, he and I continued to work on the draft. Meanwhile, I kept hearing backlash about the error. There wasn't much I could say. It was fixed and I was moving on. They were expecting the book to be a blockbuster. It was going to make the agent's career. It was going to make the editor's career. It was going to make Jim famous.

Finally, in January, my agent called to inform me that I had been removed from the project. Without telling me of their plan, she and this editor had gone to the publisher's legal department and labeled me a plagiarist, and asked to replace me with another writer. My agent admitted to me privately that she knew it was an honest mistake, but said she had to save her own reputation. I had no opportunity to defend myself.

It didn't seem real. After all, I had worked ten months on this book. I had the entire story in rough draft form and it just needed finishing. It was my baby. I was in shock at first. But as the dreadful reality started to hit – they really were hiring this other writer, they really were leaving me out in the cold, they really were not going to pay me the advance – I began to panic.

I went to Jim, asking him to do something. I had done nothing wrong. I had written four books already and never copied a word. He just basically shrugged me off. "Sorry. I asked them twice to keep you on. They said no. I don't know what to tell you."

"We're a team," I said. "Let's go back to one of the other publishers who made an offer on this project. Forget this one. They have no understanding of the subject matter to begin with."

But he was offered full credit for the story if he stayed. He was paying the other writer a flat fee. He wouldn't have to share copyright or royalties. He didn't need me anymore.

I had no legal recourse. My money was all gone, and they knew it. The advance that I was promised, half of the five figures, wasn't coming. I had no income to show for ten months of work – and I had invested my life savings.

It was too much for me. I was waking up in the middle of the night in a cold sweat, feeling as though I had been running. I couldn't do art work. My hands would not stop shaking. I was so depressed by this colossal betrayal, deeply troubled by the callousness of people, stunned by how easily they could ruin my life, and terrified for myself and my animals. I was kicking myself for trusting like this, for believing and depending on others to the extent that they could destroy me. I had thought they were my friends. I felt their actions were defrauding the story's beautiful message, which was about love, loyalty and reciprocity. I went back over the error again and again in my mind, trying to remember how it had played out, and why I had been so careless. My book, now a complete manuscript, would never be shared with the world. But perhaps worst of all, my belief in myself and my work had been violated. I always thought that if I put forward my best effort, and really gave with a willing heart, then the same would come back to me. I struggled with this concept. I felt like my very foundation had been shaken. All these agonizing thoughts were spinning through my head, night and day. It was unbearable.

Then, Trudy foundered.

I found her in her stall, standing as if frozen to the ground, leaning backward, afraid to move her feet. Dr. Cawley came out and wrapped her two front feet in heavy bandages. We put her on Bute, and I started her on the stem cell supplement that had helped Clifford so much. Within a few days, Trudy seemed a little more comfortable. She still wasn't her flexible self, but much better. Dr. Cawley had said she could go outside if she was better off the Bute, but I decided not to do that since x rays were still pending. I just wanted to find out how bad it was before I did anything.

But I did take her out for a walk in the snow. Everything was grey, with light flakes falling gently. Trudy was so happy and grateful! She arched her neck and purred softly, looking eagerly around and smelling the air.

I turned Clifford loose and he followed us down the driveway, shadowed closely by Ms. Rip. He curled his tail up over his back, snorted and took off, cavorting and bucking his way through the knee-high drifts. I wished I had my camera!

We paused and I said, "Clifford!" But he was too wrapped up in his antics to notice. I took my glove off and held it up. "Do you want to fetch my glove?"

That was all he needed to hear. He turned and came trotting over and assumed the position: Head down, ears forward, waiting for the pitch! I threw the glove and he leaped in the air, ran to it and picked it up. He came trotting back with that glove flapping in his mouth, rolling his eyes and swinging his head so the fingers waved at me.

I stood still for a minute, and then I started to laugh. I laughed and laughed. I fell down in the snow laughing.

And then, I cried. I cried for the tremendous loss of Kimmy, the tragedy of Cajun, the greed and corruption of the publishing industry. I cried for the loss of Jim and my agent, two people I had grown to love as friends. I cried because there seemed no end in sight to my financial worries and I knew I was going to lose the farm. I cried because I couldn't help take care of my parents or Amanda. I cried for the exploitation of my refuge, Clifford's Bay. And I cried for my darling Scorch, who I missed every single day, who had so bravely marched forward to his fate, who had given all that he could, only to have the cancer win.

I was afraid that to be bombarded like this; the accusations, the betrayal, the cumulative tremendous loss, could cause me to be financially and emotionally crippled for life. I was afraid that I might never recover. I worried that my reputation, my career might be ruined. I worried about public humiliation, since I had sent press releases and announcements to everyone I knew, that I had made this huge book deal.

"I think it is terrible what they did to you," my friend Liz said. "It might take me six or seven years to recover from something like this."

I didn't want to be forever scarred by this awful phase. I didn't even want to wait through six or seven years. I was walking around like a ghost, a mere shadow of my former self. My humor was gone. My ambition was gone. I didn't want to be this hopeless loser, but I didn't know who I was anymore.

Ms. Rip was nudging me frantically, pawing at me, trying to get me to stop crying. I could not stop. Lying there in the snow, completely devastated, I understood the concept of "rock bottom."

Then, I heard a soft "plop". The glove had been dropped, and it was lying in the snow right next to my face. I looked up to see Clifford standing over me. He was waiting.

I had to get up.

Chapter Eighteen

Every great inspiration is but an experiment.
~ Charles Ives

Michigan's economy was the worst in the nation. I was feeling more and more desperate as spring eased into summer, and there were no jobs to be had. Four months had gone by, and I hadn't been able to resolve my dispute with the publisher over my book project. I felt invisible, insignificant, used and very angry. My ten months of work the year before meant nothing to these people. They had simply taken my story and gone on with it, leaving me in a state of financial devastation.

One sunny afternoon, as I was working on a watercolor, an idea came to me that I thought may be a stroke of genius. I had seen an elephant on YouTube, painting a picture. Why not teach Clifford how to paint?

Who knows how much a horse's art could be worth!

It only took a few minutes to get the necessary items together: A couple of sponges, some little plastic tubs, a big pad of paper, a bunch of tubes of watercolors, my video camera, a clicker, and of course, the essential peppermints.

Clifford was just hanging out in the barn, swishing his tail and staying out of the sun. He nickered when I came in. I threw my art gear down in the aisle and grabbed his halter. I slid his door open and put the halter on him. "We're gonna try something new! Now is your chance to save the day!"

He came out, eager to see what I was so excited about. I left him standing in the aisle and I filled my little tubs with water. I took a sponge and squeezed a little color on it. I lay it on the pad of paper, which was open on the floor.

"Pick it up," I told him.

He willingly picked the sponge up, and then slurped the whole thing into his mouth as he chewed on it thoughtfully. Finally, he turned and tried to give it to me.

"No," I took it, but he didn't get clicked for that. I put it back on the paper. It hadn't made a single mark yet. "You have to just push it around. It's a painting, see? You're learning to paint."

He pawed at the pad of paper, whacking it with his foot and sending it flying.

"No!" I screeched. I ran and picked it up and laid it down again. "Just stand there, okay? Just stand there and paint."

He looked at me. I looked at him. He picked the sponge up again and I clicked him for it. I realized I had to reinforce him using his lips, not his feet.

When he heard the click, he immediately dropped the sponge and it splattered on the paper, making a beautiful violet pattern.

"Yes!" I squealed. I quickly unwrapped a peppermint and he sucked it into his mouth and then crunched it thoughtfully.

"Okay," I said. "Try again."

After all those years of retrieving, his compulsion to deliver the sponge was pretty strong. But finally he learned to just stand still and nudge it around on the paper. Pretty soon, he was getting very good at it. He learned to flip and roll the sponge, to make all kinds of interesting lines and patterns. And, he really liked to do it. However, at times he became frustrated and gave the sponge a toss, much as a human artist would! I was trying to let each layer dry completely, so that he didn't muddy the colors up. Doing watercolors this way took a lot of concentration on both our parts. I'd never produced abstract art, and I thought Clifford's work was vastly more interesting than anything abstract I would have come up with. It was fascinating to me.

I saved the first painting for Dad, but I put the second one on eBay. I posted a link to the YouTube video, to prove that Clifford was actually the artist. I went on the internet and told everyone I knew that Clifford was painting pictures. He became an instant phenomenon. His work appeared on the front page of the Wordpress website, and remained there for three days!

I called a local equestrian art gallery where some of my work was displayed, to tell her about Clifford, the amazing painting horse.

"Not a paint horse," I said. "A paint ING horse."

"Oh, thanks, but I am not taking on any new artists right now. But it's so cute that he does that," she said.

I was contacted by the organizer of the Mid-A Morgan Horse Show silent auction, asking for me to donate art or books.

"How about one of Clifford's paintings? He's so talented!" I enthused.

"Uhmm. I don't think that will work. But it is so great to see how you can enjoy art with your horse. Any other ideas?" she said.

The eBay auction passed without a single bid. Everyone was always asking to see Clifford's new art, but nobody actually wanted to buy it.

"I feel your pain, buddy," I told him. "I guess it's back to the drawing board."

I had heard of things like this helping someone to recover from a devastating loss. Animals can be terrific inspiration. Clifford definitely added an element of cheer to my days, but the thing I was beginning to understand was that it was his love for me that buoyed me. His character and wit were amplified most when he was trying to get my attention. That too, was his motive for painting. I thought he didn't do it so much for peppermints as for the fact that it was something we could do together. He loved the interaction.

It still remains to be seen whether his work is worth any more than mine.

Chapter Nineteen

So long as the memory of certain beloved friends
lives in my heart, I shall say that life is good.
~Helen Keller

In July, I found a foreclosure notice taped to my front door. With no savings, and no advance, and no royalties to promise to creditors, I couldn't pay the mortgage. The farm was as good as gone.

It had been four years since Clifford and Trudy had visited the Drummond camp. It would be temporary home for them until I could find a more permanent solution to their displacement.

My truck, being a lease, was no more. I had no way to haul them, and they couldn't travel together in Wheelzebub anyway. My friend Vickie hauled them the six hours up to Drummond for me.

Upon arriving at camp, they took a moment to look around before stepping out of the trailer. Then, despite the fact that they were both completely free, they marched directly into the corral, which was lush with grass and daisies, having been horse-free for four years.

Clifford and Trudy walked around checking things out, and then immediately they each dropped and rolled. Their obvious comfort was a comfort to me.

We took long walks on the days that followed. I walked the horses as if they were dogs. I would lead one and let the other run along with us. Clifford loved to be at liberty. Whenever we came to the fork in the road leading to Clifford's Bay, he would run down the road past the stand of birch trees, and then look invitingly back over his shoulder.

"We're not going down there," I would lead Trudy in the other direction, and Clifford would turn and come flying after us. I had heard rumors that the bay was now, "A mess," and, "Terrible."

I didn't want to look. It would be just too painful.

It had been four years since I had ridden Clifford in the Drummond Island Fourth of July parade, the year when Scorch had last accompanied us. But Clifford never forgot the routine. I trailered him down to a spot close to the starting point, where the floats and crowds were gathering along the roadside. There were plenty of horse-eating monsters there, including lots of balloons and banners and streamers galore. We expected to meet our cousins, Tess and Allen and the usual group of equines.

146

When I arrived at the spot, I realized I had grabbed Trudy's bridle by mistake. There was no way that would fit Clifford, at least not without a lot of oil to get the buckle unhooked and readjusted. I had my English saddle, a nice Ortho-flex with a blue pad. But I had no bridle, so had to ride him with just his purple halter and a too-short lead rope. I decided to skip the saddle too.

I climbed on bareback, and we were off. Clifford happily trotted down the road between all the horse-eating floats, eagerly looking forward to our rendezvous with horsey friends that he hadn't seen in years.

But we got to the grassy spot along the water's edge where the equine parade members usually gather, and nobody was there. He looked up the road from whence they usually appeared. Nothing.

"Looks like it's you and me this year, buddy," I said. I gave him a pat on the neck.

Traditionally, horses go along in front of the ambulance, and I tried to put Clifford there. But he immediately fell in behind a Charlie Brown float that was playing the "Linus and Lucy" theme song. I wondered if he remembered this tune. It had been our theme song during a couple of his performances at the

Novi Expo, years ago.

There were some little kids in line behind us that were carrying a big white poster board sign and some balloons. When the parade started, they decided to run and shout, dashing up right near Clifford's tail. This proved too much for him and he startled. They didn't seem to notice and just kept coming! Finally I called back to them, "Hey you guys, you're scaring my horse!"

They slowed down to a walk then, but still wanted to be right on top of us. I said, "Can you stay back a little? This parade just moves really slowly."

They did fall back then and gave us plenty of room. I just didn't want anyone to get under his feet by accident, or even get whacked by his tail.

He seemed very happy to just walk along behind that float in time to the piano music. He was doing so well that I reached down to attempt to untie the lead rope from his halter. Every time I reached for it he would playfully turn his head and lip at my fingers.

Finally I ended up just dropping the lead rope and scratching his withers as we walked along. A couple of girls cried out to me, "Wow! Is he bullet proof, or what?"

"I guess as much as any horse can be bullet proof," I replied.

I was remembering the day before, when I had received a call from my friend Rita in Ann Arbor, saying that one of her employees wanted to buy Clifford!

I said, "What? Clifford's not for sale!"

She said that this person claimed my website said I was having him put to sleep!

That, of course, was ludicrous. So, I was thinking about this on our little parade walk, after I had dropped the lead rope and was just a passenger on his back, scratching him on the withers. We had been together sixteen years and there was just no explaining, or emulating, this kind of connection. I didn't know why a rumor this absurd would ever fly. The only thing I could think of is that our hard times might be causing people to jump to some sad conclusions.

When we got to the end, I turned to the kids behind me and said, "Thanks, guys. You did a great job."

They smiled proudly.

I remembered my first time in the parade, some fifteen years prior, when Clifford was still a youngster.

Allen Hoey was riding Barney, his grey Arabian, bareback. I thought I would never see the day when I'd be riding any horse in a parade with no saddle. On this day, Clifford had shown me that I could achieve the unexpected.

The message is clear: If you persevere, one day you may surprise yourself.

Traditionally, after the parade I took the horses down to Clifford's Bay. Our last jaunt was the day, four years prior, when Clifford had leaped over Scorch.

Something was pulling me back there. Perhaps it was a morbid sort of curiosity, perhaps it was just the fact that I thought Cliffy might like to roll in the sand.

I thought of the big buck I had smacked with the car, sprawling on the road, and then struggling to his feet. I thought of the tattered butterfly. And I thought of my brother, Jon, who had walked away from the rehab center just days after regaining the use of his legs.

"That's what life is like, Nancy," he had said later. "There are good days, and bad days. There are ups and downs."

I was grateful that he was able to tell me this. I still had Jon. I still had Clifford and Trudy. Maybe it was time I learned the meaning of, "The wisdom to know the difference."

When we got back to camp, I saddled up Trudy and rode her up the hill past the old sawmill. Clifford trotted happily ahead of us, stopping here and there at the road's edge, tearing and chomping at the grass. Ms. Rip, my only remaining dog, followed along.

We trotted through the woods, through the dappled shadows of the ancient cedars. This time, when Clifford trotted ahead at the fork in the road, we followed him. We turned down the rocky, rugged two-track that led through the cedar swamp and the maple hardwood. We passed a big sign that said, "Lots for Sale." We passed some "Private Property" signs and a rickety wooden fence. Clifford broke into a lope then, plunging around the corner where the trees parted to reveal the sandy shoreline. I pulled Trudy up as Clifford went tearing down to the beach with Ripple close on his heels. The shore was torn up, the sand tracked in high, hard ridges from someone driving on it. The water level was completely changed, much higher, murky now, with tall, wild swamp grass growing everywhere.

But the sun gleamed on the smooth water's surface, and a solid, unspoiled wall of cedar trees still remained on either shore. The grassy banks were dotted with bright orange Indian paintbrushes. A noisy group of terns flapped over the inlet. Clifford galloped along the water's edge, kicking up tracks in the hard white sand, and then stopped and turned to look back at us with an exultant snort.

I drew a deep sigh, a huge relief. Beneath all the scars, it was still there, just as it had always been.

About the Author

Originally from Michigan's beautiful Upper Peninsula, Nancy has been writing stories about animals since she was a child. She is also an accomplished artist, and her award-winning work has been sought by collectors worldwide. *Clifford's Bay* is Nancy's sixth book. She is a budding screenwriter, and an award-winning playwright. She shares her life with a bevy of pets, including an inimitable Morgan horse named Clifford.

CPSIA information can be obtained
at www.ICGtesting.com
Printed in the USA
LVOW04s2207280716
498238LV00033B/789/P